The Pilgrim Psalms

Our Pilgrimage to God's Presence

Jimmy R. Reagan

Copyright © 2017, 2022 Jimmy R. Reagan
(Minor Revisions in 2022)
All rights reserved. No part of this book may be reproduced, stored in a retrieval system, or transmitted in any form or by any means—electronic, mechanical, photocopy, recording, or otherwise—without written permission of the author, except for brief quotations in printed reviews.
ISBN: 978-1973850397

DEDICATION

To Gerald and Pat Reagan

CONTENTS

	Preface	7
1	**Introduction**	9
2	**Psalm 120** Woe Is Me	13
3	**Psalm 121** I Will Lift Up Mine Eyes unto the Hills	21
4	**Psalm 122** Let Us Go unto The House of The Lord	29
5	**Psalm 123** Until	37
6	**Psalm 124** The Lord Who Was on Our Side	45
7	**Psalm 125** As Mount Zion	51
8	**Psalm 126** Like Them That Dream	57
9	**Psalm 127** Labor in Vain	63
10	**Psalm 128** Blessed Is Everyone That Feareth The Lord	73
11	**Psalm 129** Many a Time Have They Afflicted Me	81
12	**Psalm 130** Out of the Depths	89
13	**Psalm 131** Things Too High for Me	97
14	**Psalm 132** Lord Remember	105
15	**Psalm 133** Unity	113
16	**Psalm 134** Bless the Lord	121
17	**Conclusion**	129

PREFACE

It's hard to imagine how the Pilgrim Psalms are so little known. Though they are covered by all the great commentaries on the Book of Psalms, very few volumes have ever been written about them exclusively. By comparison, you can find several titles written on the Messianic Psalms. The Pilgrim Psalms may very well be the most deeply effective in fostering personal fellowship with the Lord amid the troubles of life to be found in the entire Old Testament. If you are not yet impressed by these Pilgrim Psalms, it could only mean that you haven't carefully studied them yet. My prayer is that this book will serve as a little encouragement for God's people to immerse themselves in the Pilgrim Psalms and reap their incredible spiritual benefits.

I've had the privilege of studying and preaching through these Pilgrim Psalms in both of my pastorates, in Ohio and South Carolina, respectively. As a preacher scanning the faces of those in the congregation, I've had these psalms amaze me in their ability to speak to where people live. There might be two or three of these Pilgrim Psalms that you especially need today, but you will need the rest of them soon enough. I can confess their personal help to me.

I'd like to dedicate this book to my parents, Gerald and Pat Reagan. Their unconditional and steadfast love for me has enriched my life beyond my ability to express. My mother led me to Jesus and challenged me to make Him the focus of my life. My father loved me and spent time with me in a generation where most fathers had no time for their sons. They did their very best for me and I have been incredibly blessed by it. I dearly love them both.

My library is full of books that have helped me grasp these wonderful Pilgrim Psalms, yet the final product that you hold in your hands is mine imperfections and all.

My prayer is that this book will encourage Christians on their Christian pilgrimage as well as help my fellow laborers who teach and preach God's Word. God bless!

1

INTRODUCTION

The fifteen psalms from Psalm 120 to 134 have come to be known as the Pilgrim Psalms. The Bible paints a portrait across its pages of believers being pilgrims in this world. Every Christian should see him- or herself as a pilgrim passing through this world and traveling to a better place that will finally be home. On this pilgrimage, we have our struggles. As is often said, this world is no friend of grace. No wonder the book of Hebrews adds to the idea by calling us *"pilgrims and strangers"*.

Despite what awaits us at the end of this pilgrimage, we grapple with a host of issues that hinders us from the presence of the God to Whom we travel. Our pilgrimage becomes ever more wearying unless we learn to unload these heavy issues from off our backs to travel on to His presence. In His graciousness, the Lord has given us these Pilgrim Psalms.

Having these Pilgrim Psalms collected in one place in the Psalter is rather unusual as groupings of similar psalms go. For example, Messianic Psalms are found in various places in the Book of Psalms with no discernable pattern. The Pilgrim Psalms are clearly unique in the collection of Psalms our Lord has given us in the beloved Book of Psalms.

Each of these psalms has the heading *"Song of Degrees."* *"Degrees"* is defined as "ascent, steps, or a going up." There are a variety of theories among scholars about what these degrees mean. Some take the meaning "steps" and think it refers to 15 steps ascending the Temple. There are plenty of reasons to believe that is not the case. We are never told that there were exactly these fifteen steps at the Temple, nor is it likely that Pilgrims would overflow these steps singing on each of these psalms. We have no historical information that such activities took place on the Temple steps.

A much more likely scenario is that these psalms were sung by traveling Pilgrims making their way to Jerusalem from all parts of Israel to worship at the Temple. Days of travel would give a much more plausible opportunity to sing and meditate on these special psalms. You will notice as you read these Pilgrim Psalms that sometimes a soloist sings while at other times it's the entire choir, or band of pilgrims. We know that the Jewish people traveled to Jerusalem for the three major feasts each year: 1) **Passover** [spring], 2) **Pentecost** [early summer], and 3) **Tabernacles** [fall]. The Bible tells us that these pilgrims sang enroute to pass time on the journey (Psalm 42:4, Isaiah 30:29).[1] There are other Scriptures showing an ascent to either the Tabernacle or Temple: I Samuel 1:3 and Isaiah 2:3 as well as in the Pilgrim Psalms themselves (Psalm 122:4). Make sure you visualize the scene in your mind—Pilgrims traveling on foot and interrupting their lives to travel to God's Holy City.

No matter which way they traveled to Jerusalem they would have to ascend at some point as Jerusalem is among hills. Since God dwelt then in His Shekinah Glory in the Temple, this pilgrimage had everything to do with going to the presence of God. These psalms are timeless treasures to God's children in that we all travel to God's presence. We no longer travel to physical Jerusalem, but we do go to worship Him. Like them, we are often weary pilgrims as we go. They often traveled together in groups as there were so many possibilities of trouble in travel of those days. We also must realize that our struggles are often in common with other believers. We, too, have much opposition as we travel to God's presence.

The Pilgrims of those days (and these pilgrimages lasted through the earthly ministry of Jesus Christ) always involved getting to that Temple, or before its completion, the Tabernacle. Since God dwelt there, there was no other acceptable place to go. Though

---

[1] Because the requirement to travel to Jerusalem for these feasts was only laid upon males, we will refer to the pilgrim throughout as "he" or "him".

different now, we ascend spiritually to the Lord in prayer, in the fellowship of communion, and worship whether private or corporately in church. The point of these psalms is that the pilgrim has many distractions that derail going into the presence of the Lord. They might keep walking and get to Jerusalem, but their hearts would not be where they should be for something as sublime as God's presence. Again, we can walk aimlessly as we have no physical Jerusalem to reach, but those inward problems that mar going into His presence plague us today as much as in any generation.

Though these psalms cover a variety of issues that trouble our pilgrimage, they display some clear similarities. Each psalm individually contains a full thought worthy of a pilgrim's time to sing and dwell on. Beyond that individuality, many have noticed that there appears to be five sets of 3 psalms here too. Each set seems to begin with some element of distress or trouble followed by an exercise in realizing truth and trusting in God. Each cycle then ends with a clear display of triumph.

The final unique feature of this collection of psalms is that you can see a discernable progress to Jerusalem. Psalm 120 begins at a distance farthest away, and then we proceed to see the hills of Jerusalem, followed by seeing the Temple, and finally entering the gates and reaching the presence of the Lord. Apparently, they linger near the Temple before entering. Think of these 15 Pilgrim Psalms as steps to God's presence with the last step being the arrival where we can finally bless the Lord.

One of the greatest needs of our lives, to say nothing of our eternity, is to have the presence of the Lord. Because of its immense value, we must take heed to the multiple tripping points on the way to it. We were made for His presence and can never have peace without it. To work through, then, the issues that obscure the Presence from us should be considered one of the paramount issues of us life. To aid us in that critical task, the Lord in His vast lovingkindness has given us these Pilgrim Psalms.

The Pilgrim Ascends In the Pilgrim Psalms

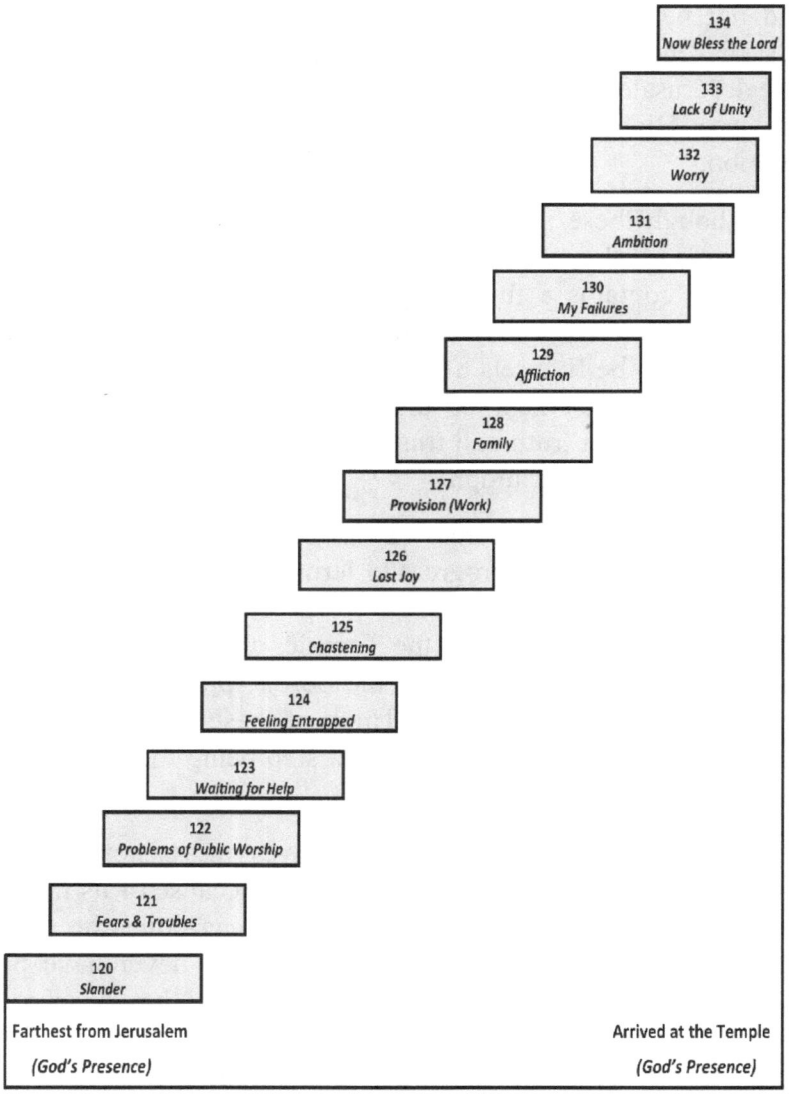

2

WOE IS ME

Psalm 120

Are you distressed? Has someone hurt you? Is the distress such that it is even affecting you in going on to the Lord's presence? Is it affecting you either in private or at church? Perhaps the hurt sprang from slander, but it's really crippling your spiritual life. We should, then, look at this first of the Pilgrim Psalms as it tells us what to do when all we feel like saying is *"Woe is me."*

I. Remembering the Lord (v.1)

A. My Distress

The pilgrimage begins here in the Pilgrim Psalms. The heading *"A Song of Degrees"* begins this psalm as it does in every one of the fifteen Pilgrim Psalms. *"Degrees"* here means "an ascent, or a going up." The idea in these psalms is that the pilgrims traveling to Jerusalem are going to the very presence of God at the Temple. These travelers would sing these psalms as they would go along the winding roads of Israel. These songs match the very problems that hinder us from getting to the presence of our Lord. Like these ancient pilgrims traveled to Jerusalem to God's presence, we ascend spiritually to our Lord in prayer, fellowship, or even worship whether in private or in a church setting.

In this first Pilgrim Psalm, these pilgrims are the farthest away from Jerusalem. To find our application, we are at that place, wherever it is, that is farthest away from His presence. Even though we notice this distance, let's not misjudge these pilgrims. They want to reach Jerusalem and the presence of the Lord even if they are facing these difficulties. We can see ourselves here as those who truly love the Lord and sincerely want to make our way into His presence even if we find it a struggle. These travelers aren't fakes, but true pilgrims who find the way challenging.

In this psalm, we see a serious cry of distress from the Psalmist. Since we aren't told until verse 2 that this distress is about slander and being lied on, we realize that the principles of this psalm really apply to any distress. This first Pilgrim Psalm, even if it comes to tell us of a specific problem, wants us to see that the real problem is being kept away from the presence of the Lord. The problems that hinder us in the first place are secondary to the vital issue of being close to, or abiding in, our Lord.

Of all things, why would these pilgrims sing about such an unpleasant subject as they travel to Jerusalem? Even melancholy people who sing the Blues in our day typically sing about trouble in general, or someone else's trouble, not the trouble really laying them low. We tend to try to force such personally sad subjects out of our minds, but here we seem to see such singing praised. Why?

We must acknowledge that these troubling issues are something that must be dealt with or the whole idea of going into the Lord's presence will be sabotaged. Since there is a path beyond them, or at least help through them, these painful issues must be drug out before our eyes. Those who don't will likely never get to the presence of the Lord. Being consumed with *"my distress"* will hinder me from meaningful worship, worship of the only One Who can help that distress, so, of course, I must deal with it!

The distressed pilgrim must bring it out into the open of his heart so his mind won't be all tied up in knots when he should be making his way into the Lord's presence. This problem is equally true for you and me as we are on our way to church or the prayer closet. Have you ever gone to the place of prayer about your problems only to sink deeper into your problems and totally forget you were talking to the Lord? Have you had your prayer time devolve into a pointless pity time when it was the Lord's help you so desperately needed? Have you ever gone to church and could never get out of your troubled thought life enough to worship the Lord in a meaningful way? These are not the ways to get help! Distress should help us seek the Lord, not hinder us from it. We need to sing as a Christian pilgrim and deal with these issues in some way. We need to leave these troubles behind and go on to the Lord.

B. His Hearing

Dealing with these distresses seems easier said than done, but we have something to draw on—the Lord's track record with us. We've been through distresses before, and the Lord has always gotten us through them. That fact ought to pull the thought of dealing with our distresses on the way to the Lord's presence out of the impossible category.

The Pilgrim Psalmist in his distress said, "*I cried unto the LORD, and he heard me.*" "*Cried*" means "called", and so in other words, he's saying, "I prayed, and He heard me." This experience is the expected lot of all believers following the Lord. If that is an experience you know nothing of, then your problems are deeper than that of a weary yet believing Pilgrim. On the other hand, there's facts here the pilgrim must not overlook. Because we have His Word, and because we know what He has done in the past, we really should trust what He will do in our current situation. Those conclusions should help us endure until in His time He delivers us.

Don't miss that the Pilgrim Psalmist said, "*he heard me.*" What a sweet truth! To call on the Lord is always the right move. The truth is that asking us to deal with these distresses as we come to worship Him is simply to have faith that He hasn't suddenly lost the power to do what He has always done.

II. Facing My Problem (v. 2-4)

A. My Hurt

The idea is that I can deal with my problem because I remember God. To see the attempt in getting this fixed, or to see the way to the Lord, notice the improvement from "*distress*" (verse 1) to "*deliver*" (verse 2). We don't know for sure the event being discussed here, but many conjecture that this episode is Doeg's attack on David (I Samuel 22). So, David, or whomever the Psalmist was, is saying, I need deliverance from slander and malicious lies. Though verse 1 could refer to any general distress, this psalm narrows its focus to a specific distress that hurts deeply—the barbs of slander.

The Psalmist is saying he craves escape. He screams from his heart, "Lies have been told on me; Someone's tongue is full of deceit." It's so bad that the passage says, "*lying lips*", "*deceitful tongue*", and "*false tongue*" so that the horror of it would not be missed. As you probably have personally experienced at some point, slander is particularly difficult because it's so hard to defend yourself against. Slander hides in private corners spoken by shadowy figures. You likely will never even have the story's facts, or who all has told it, or who all has heard it, to even know exactly how to respond.

History has taught us that slander rarely stops with words but turns uglier and descends into fights and violence. It's been known to rear its putrid head in businesses, workplaces, families, communities, and even churches. The pain can so sidetrack us that we forget praying for the help we need. Slander is especially piercing to the godly because their testimony means so much to them, and as that slander damages what they hold so dear. Yes, these lying lips can really stir the pot of trouble.

B. His Vengeance

The Pilgrim Psalmist asked the question we would like to ask here. Though he isn't talking to the slanderers, he does want to know what's going to be given to them (verse 3). He's really asking, what will the Lord do? Haven't you thought the same questions before? In his questioning, he pronounced a true spiritual principle – those who slander will find the greatest hurt to be that which comes back on themselves. That spiritual principle brings the true solution to light. Leave it to the Lord!

Retribution will come, but we pilgrims are not to try to help it along. You can speak the truth, but don't try to set the matter straight by revenge. Retaliation only drops you to the level of the slanderers and you may get worked up and start slandering yourself. Just remember that is far better to be slandered than to be a slanderer. Far better, too, because there is a God Who judges slander.

"*Sharp arrows*" evoke that the tongue's damage was like a warrior's fierce arrow. On the other hand, the Lord's arrows will reach where the other arrows never could. "*Coals of juniper*", from broom bushes, are a perfect comparison because they burn hotter, last longer, and even reignite more easily. That suggests the idea of being hot longer and therefore being more painful. These comparisons demand we answer a question. Since your revenge could never be as effective as His vengeance, why go there? In any event, you don't put out a fire with more heat; for that you need cold water.

I don't have to worry about vengeance because God is

This line of thinking reminds us of the more famous passage in Romans 12:19-21: "*Dearly beloved, avenge not yourselves, but rather give place unto wrath: for it is written, Vengeance is mine; I will repay, saith the Lord. Therefore if thine enemy hunger, feed him; if he thirst, give him drink: for in so doing thou shalt heap coals of fire on his head. Be not overcome of evil, but overcome evil with good.*" The point is that we should be careful about those hot words as they may be coming back down on our own heads.

III. Giving My Problems to God (v. 5-7)

A. My Surrounding

Although the pilgrim asked the Lord for help in dealing with this slander, he still bursts forth in verse 5 with "*woe is me*". Have you ever felt this way? Have you ever blurted out those same words? Does *"woe is me"* describe an attitude that had enveloped your thinking? If you are like me, or the pilgrim in this Psalm, I imagine it has.

"Woe is me" is not the best attitude for one who loves the Lord, so we are being called on to deal with it. It's why the pilgrim sings. It's why the Lord records it in this Psalm. This world system isn't geared toward Christians, so naturally you will not always feel comfortable here. It's to be expected. For that matter, you can't be comfortable in the middle of slander either.

Verse 5 mentions two places that the pilgrim has sojourned. Mesech is an area north of Israel near the Black Sea while Kedar is to the southeast among a vicious desert-roaming people. These two places are too far apart for a pilgrim to be dwelling at both, so they must be representing something else. In fact, they are two opposite directions and remind us that trouble can come at us from multiple directions at one time. The pilgrim is among barbarians. Clearly, the idea is that the pilgrim here is the farthest from Jerusalem that he will be, or more importantly, the farthest from the presence of God. In this first Pilgrim Psalm, we are the farthest distance away. No wonder this is the time the pilgrim said, *"woe is me"*.

When you read regarding these barbaric places, *"sojourn"*, *"dwell"*, and *"long dwelt"*, you realize the mess this pilgrim is in. Since a pilgrim is a traveler, we see the ongoing nature of this problem. Verse 6 suggests that this pilgrim has been around a long time in this place where he is. A wise pilgrim realizes that this will often be his lot until he is home. Likewise, we modern-day pilgrims will face the struggles of this unfriendly world until we reach Heaven itself.

When the pilgrim says in verse 7, *"I am for peace"*, he is really saying that he hates fighting, but those he deals with love it and reject all overtures of peace. They ignore every honest attempt at peace, and always return to hostility. Again, this comes as no surprise in our day as we remember this world has already rejected the Prince of Peace. This world fights Christ, Who is our peace. No doubt this is tiring but remember you're a pilgrim and this world is not your home.

B. His Lesson

When you think more deeply about verses 6 and 7, the pilgrim should see that it is his duty to speak for peace. It is no accident that the word *"peace"* is mentioned twice in these two verses. God's people are always called to seek peace and pursue it (Psalms 34:14).

Don't let the apparent lack of resolution fool you. There's more guidance here than you might think. In verses 2-7, the pilgrim vented briefly as is often needed at times, but clearly, he is reaching out to the Lord. Maybe you figured out by now that you can't make people do anything, but you can take it to the Lord. Here in the Pilgrim Psalm farthest away from Jerusalem you do find the least resolution.[2] What can't be ignored is that slander is hard to fix, but verse 1 is still the right approach. The pilgrim must pray, sing, and cry out to the Lord as he travels along. That's the way to go happily to Jerusalem, or the place of prayer, or to the church for worship, or into the very presence of God. Leave it on the side of the road, pilgrim, and head on to Jerusalem as that is all you can do with "*Woe is me.*"

---

[2] **Psalm 123 is similar in apparent unresolved resolution.**

3

I Will Lift Up Mine Eyes unto The Hills

Psalm 121

Are you scared about tomorrow? Do all the uncertainties and worries of life really get to you? Do you at times imagine all the awful things that could happen to you? Do the thoughts of these things cloud your mind and heart as you approach the presence of the Lord? Dear Pilgrim, it is time for you to say, "*I will lift up mine eyes unto the hills?*"

I. The Lord Helps Me (v. 1-2)

A. I Need Helping

The pilgrim walks along with his whole journey ahead of him, and in the distance, views the hills on which sits the holy city of God, Jerusalem. In Psalm 120 the pilgrim had to stop and deal with problems (in that case slander) that hindered him from going joyfully to the presence of the Lord. In this Psalm, we find that problems and fears associated with what lies ahead could hinder or worry us, as well. Perhaps as he makes camp, he sees the last gentle rays of the sun faintly illumine these hills. God is there and fellowship and communion await.

In those swirling thoughts of fear, the pilgrim would naturally think of the help he needed on this journey. He glances upwards toward the hills as he thinks of this needed assistance. Since these hills meet the sky, we naturally lift our eyes to see its beauty. As one who grew up in the Smoky Mountains, how well I can reflect on drinking in the view of the mountains and my eyes following them up to where they meet the skies. That careful look is good, too, as upward is the way a pilgrim's eyes should always look.

In Psalm 120 he tells us of dwelling in Mesech and Kedar, which were pictures of barbaric places, and that is where he will be returning when he comes back from Jerusalem. In addition, there's also the danger of all he left exposed at home while he is on this journey. All males 20 and up were to go to these three feasts and most obeyed. That made for a dangerous situation at home that he had to leave in the Lord's hands. If that weren't bad enough, there were cases of the pilgrim leaving his wife and children, his sick or elderly parents, and certainly some of his best property.

Beyond the dangers back at home, there's the perils of the journey. A band of thieves could be around any corner, sunstrokes could come from those long, hot hours on the trail, and an accident like falling off one of the high cliffs was always a distinct possibility. Of course, if the enemies out there that are stronger than you, naturally you think about the help you'll need and where it will come from. The pilgrim's mind is consumed with what his problems may grow into, or what other dangers lurk ahead in a world so fraught with disaster, a world where we are so helpless and unable to conquer in our own strength. Just like that ancient pilgrim, our uncertainty is our greatest fear – the fear of what will happen tomorrow. We pilgrims of today carry the exact same worries.

B. He Ever Helps

Some interpret verse 1 as some sort of teaching on worshiping nature, but that's a complete interpretive misfire. Jeremiah 3:23 says, *"Truly in vain is salvation hoped for from the hills, and from the multitude of mountains: truly in the LORD our God is the salvation of Israel."* Further, we have verse 2 to keep our interpretation in line. The point of the lifting up of his eyes toward Jerusalem is that he immediately is led to think of the Maker of those hills. The point is not really looking at Jerusalem, but as your eyes rise they keep looking up to Heaven where the Lord dwells. It's as if he says, look up at those hills! My help comes from that direction! In verse 2 he is saying, let me get more specific – *"my help cometh from the Lord."* That help is the point here as we see *"my help"* two times in this passage. There is no other source for help. That fact every pilgrim must see.

Though it is often a point of failure, the natural cry of the Christian heart is to look upward, or in other words, to look up to God. Don't look down. There's nothing there. Don't look at self. There is even less there. For that matter, you look in vain if you look to the right or to the left, to your friend or your family. You must look up to the Lord Who is there to help you even as you wrestle with trust. May all we weary pilgrims always look up!

Yes, there are uncertainties, which we magnify, that can hinder us from coming into His presence in worship or in prayer. For many of us, it's the vicious cycle of being hindered again by fear from getting aid from the Helper and Protector and Vanquisher of fear! Pilgrim, we too must deal with the same issues on our way to our Jerusalem, which is going into His presence. So, look up Christian! There is help from the Great Helper, and as you should be excited to see, it's the very help you need. It's a help that is on time and perfect as well. It's help from the All-Powerful One. The One Who made all can easily help a band of weary pilgrims. A God Who is Creator, even of these hills, is a God sufficient to help. This calming fact the pilgrim can think of as he makes camp.

II. The Lord Keep Me (v. 3-5)

A. I Need Keeping

"He will not suffer thy foot to be moved". Wow! He's not going to allow my foot to slip. The word *"moved"* means "to slip, or slide, or stagger, or be shaken". That's simple enough. It's not only a high bluff where I may still slip and fall, but a hundred other things where I may slip and slide around and be helpless. With only a minimal review of life, we see this possibility exists for us all.

In verses 3 and 4 he gives the appearance of someone talking to himself. Unusually, in this case it's in the good way. (Perhaps the song is a solo in verses 1 and 2 that now becomes either a duet or choir singing as if talking back to the soloist). We know that a Christian may slip and slide, but here we see that we will not slip one inch more than the Lord allows. Why? I have Someone keeping me! What a glorious thought. I'm kept by the Lord! Take that, you uncertainties that race my heart!

This pilgrim is starting to catch on to something. You will notice that *"I"* and *"my"* are never said again after the first two verses. The rest of the way this pilgrim only speaks of *"The LORD"*, *"he"*, *"thee"*, or *"thy"*. That's the profound difference that being kept by the Lord makes.

I read a story of a man who decided he'd only put one word on his tombstone to summarize his life. Folks wondered what he'd use to describe himself. Do you know what word he picked? "Kept". Now that is a man that had it figured out exactly. The truth is, if I didn't need keeping, then there couldn't be uncertainties. But as it turns out, there are many uncertainties in life, and I need His keeping.

B. He Ever Keeps

In His keeping of me the traveling pilgrim, He never slumbers. In those days, men would have to keep watch at night upon the city walls for fear of invading armies. These traveling parties faced a similar danger from marauding groups or sneaky thieves and would need men to rotate keeping watch all night. The problem was that in such a caravan, all would be exhausted after a day of walking and would find it a great challenge to be an effective guard. Whether it be your turn or your fellow traveler's turn, you would fear the watchmen falling asleep. As you know, many have done that very thing. Just ask Peter, James, and John who Jesus asked three times to keep watch the night of His arrest.

The obvious problem is that you can't always watch or keep yourself; you'll have to sleep, but He'll be watching! While you fret about falling asleep, just remember that no disaster or evil will snatch you away from the Lord because He never sleeps. He never gets tired or weary or careless. He's always watching and He's always alert; He's not even drowsy. How different than the gods of Baal who Elijah faced on Mount Carmel, but our God is ever alert. Your natural fears are correct in that a human keeper may fall asleep, but those same fears are wrong in that our Great God never will.

There's great comfort in verses 4 and 5 as we see that the Lord keeps Israel and He keeps *"thee"*, which means He keeps His people, and He keeps me. In verse 5 the thought is brought out for the third time: *"The LORD is thy keeper."* The word *"thy"* is so precious in this phrase. The Lord is our shade (remember Jonah) and so is our defender. The text says specifically that He is our shade *"upon thy right hand"*, which represents the idea of the place of protection. *God is my place of protection*

This is the place where the pilgrim must think of the Lord. No thugs, dangers, or uncertainties can get to you pilgrim because He is your keeper! Again, He keeps Israel too. That means He keeps me collectively as part of the Body of Christ and He keeps me individually. *He keeps me individually*

III. The Lord Preserves Me (V. 6-8)

A. I Need Preserving

We've already seen the word *"keepeth"* that means "to hedge about" carries the idea of guarding or protecting. In the last part of the passage, it is exchanged for *"preserve"*. These two English words turn out to be the same word in Hebrew.[3] No doubt, the KJV translators want us to see the depths of meaning of this powerful word. *"Keeping"* is a word that we often associate with the here and now, but *"preserving"* suggests the future. Both aspects are true in the teaching given here in this Pilgrim Psalm.

---

[3] Together these two English words representing the same Hebrew word are in the passage six times. Clearly this word is the key of the passage.

In other words, I need keeping both now and in the future. The sun may strike me down this very day with the sun stroke, but later in the night I may get my throat sliced while I sleep. My need for protection always extends from now on into the future and shows how desperately I need preserving.

B. He Ever Preserves

Keep your eyes open to see a growing preservation as we finish out the verses in this Psalm. I must see how He meets my need for preservation. Verse 6 reminds me that He is stronger than the scorching Middle East sun; He is protection from the burning heat so dangerous to a pilgrim like me. Pilgrim, He is stronger than the problem out there that may seem scorching to you today.

We see that His preservation also extends to *"the moon by night."* Though they believed in moon stroke in those days, the idea here is poetic for all dangers of the night that a pilgrim might face. Whether it be cold, crime, darkness, fear, or any other such uncertainty, He preserves us there too. Pilgrim, He can preserve you through the painful chilly times as easily as the hot times that can smite, wither, and scorch.

In verses 7 and 8 we lose the specific and see that He has all the bases covered. When it says, *"from all evil"*, it's just the idea that we are protected from all harm. It reminds us of Romans 8:38-39: *"For I am persuaded, that neither death, nor life, nor angels, nor principalities, nor powers, nor things present, nor things to come, nor height, nor depth, nor any other creature, shall be able to separate us from the love of God, which is in Christ Jesus our Lord."* This preservation is so incredible that the Lord preserves my weak faith in *"thy soul"* – yes, we are eternally secure!

Verse 8 goes on to prove that everything is covered. When it says, *"going out"* and *"coming in"*, it suggests that I'm preserved wherever I go and whatever I do. That covers even my work, my life's tasks and toils, and the problems of the daily grind. For the pilgrim in this Psalm that will suggest coming to Jerusalem and going all the way back home. Even those problems you bring home to your haven, you are to fear not because the Lord is your doorkeeper. The *"coming in"* here is much stronger than *"whence cometh"* of verse 1. To cap it off, it says, *"and even forevermore."* He's never going to stop! He goes with us pilgrims through time and eternity, even through life and death.

I read a story of a girl, a daughter of the sea captain, who was in bed as a tremendous storm struck the ship. The storm was so bad that the ship heaved sideways and many including the girl rolled out of bed. She asked the attendant, "Is my Daddy on deck?" When he told her that her father was, she crawled back in bed and slept soundly while others panicked. She had confidence in her father. That's the same confidence we need in our Heavenly Father.

All the years of my childhood, I felt that same complete security in my Daddy's home. Never once in all those years did I ever feel I wasn't secure in the home protected by my Daddy. Still, our loving fathers might fail despite their best efforts, but our Heavenly Father, our Preserver, never will! We pilgrims are secure in our Father's hands.

Pilgrim, look up to God and go on to worship either corporately or in private. You are safe and secure! Don't be consumed by uncertainties. You have a Keeper, so sing confidently. You are preserved. Go on to Jerusalem, pilgrim! Go on to prayer, to worship, to church – lift your eyes beyond the mountains to the heavens where your Keeper dwells and help comes from. It's time today to say: *"I will lift up mine eyes unto the hills."*

4

Let Us Go into The House of the Lord

Psalm 122

What goes through your mind when it is time to go into the presence of the Lord? What are you really thinking as you delve into God's Word, or go to prayer time, or arrive at church to worship? What, really, are the feelings of your heart? That might be a question we would not particularly want to answer. Even with that natural reluctance, I think we would all agree that the answer is obvious. There's a joy that should be present, pilgrim, when we come to our Lord's presence. A joy so real that we would spontaneously say: *"Let us go into the house of the Lord."*

I. Gladness in the House of the Lord (V. 1-2)

A. Invited

As the pilgrim here opens on a note of gladness, we see that the pilgrim has dealt with the issues presented in Psalm 120 and 121.[4] In Psalm 120 we dealt with all the troubles we were already in as we began to leave to go up to the House of the Lord in Jerusalem. In Psalm 121 we dealt with troubles we thought we might encounter along the way. Now as we enter Psalm 122, with some of the other issues faced, we are ready to enter Jerusalem and the house of the Lord where worship can begin. This, of course, is the reason we came.

---

[4] That is not to suggest that there won't be more valleys for the pilgrim to traverse in these 15 Pilgrim Psalms. In fact, these Pilgrim Psalms seem to go forward in sets of three.

To get our bearings straight, we realize the primary interpretation here is the Israelite pilgrim going to the Temple in Jerusalem. In that this psalm is about the Temple, this particular Pilgrim Psalm focuses especially on the public place of God's presence. The application is obvious too. The Christian pilgrim is heading to the heavenly Jerusalem, and along the way, he also heads to the worship of the Lord here specifically in the local church.

Verse 1 begins with "*I*" to show us that one pilgrim speaks to, and for, the other pilgrims. Someone had said to him, "*Let us*" and naturally it makes him glad. For this pilgrim in David's time, as we saw in the heading "*a Song of degrees of David*", this pilgrim is going up in the latter days of David's reign when the Tabernacle is now permanently in Jerusalem. A few years later it will be the Temple. For those who want to push this Psalm to after the Exile, we should remember that there was no throne of David at that time.

In this Pilgrim Psalm, the pilgrim is a role model. Going up to God's presence to worship filled him with gladness. That is our benchmark as we approach worship – the prayer closet, the place of morning devotions, our local church – that we come with gladness as we have the extraordinary privilege to fellowship with God! This pilgrim heard "*let us go into the house of the Lord*" at home as they began to leave, likely every morning as the caravan left camp, and now finally as they stand right at the very gates of Jerusalem. This scene is the setting of this Psalm. In addition, the Pilgrim likely had precious memories of previous trips to Jerusalem while now at Jerusalem's gate, to hear a message of "come on in" was thrilling. This gladness is the expected reaction of any pilgrim who has a mighty God to worship!

Though we are only at the beginning of this Psalm, we are already at a place to examine ourselves. How do we view coming to the place of prayer to talk with our Lord? Are we glad? When we come to the quiet place to open God's Word, are we joyous? Does the morning TV news so beckon us that we would rather fellowship with the TV anchor, or a person on the television, or newspaper, or internet, who neither knows us, nor hears us, nor sees us, instead of our loving Lord?

Though this has clear application to our private worship, as we've already discussed, it is even more in this case directed at public worship. The use of the word *"us"* suggests that the assembly of believers coming to worship is a principal of God's Word, a desire of our Lord, and a clear command to us. As the famous Hebrews 10:25 says, *"Not forsaking the assembling of ourselves together, as the manner of some is; but exhorting one another: and so much the more, as ye see the day approaching."*

This pilgrim found gladness in the assembly of God's people to worship. This point so reminds me of an episode in my childhood. My pastor, Milburn White, had an elderly relative whose name I have long since forgotten visit us in the small mountain church I grew up in. His relative was feeble, his health was clearly failing, and as I recall, my pastor told us he died a few months later. In the service that morning, my pastor asked for testimonies. There was a joy on that man's face that I shall never forget as long as I live. Even at that young age, I realized that that was a Christianity worth having. Not that I yet had such a mature faith, but it was striking in that old man. His voice, suddenly buoyant and vibrant, quoted: *"I was glad when they said unto me, Let us go into the house of the Lord."* I had the privilege to know what this verse meant long before I ever even studied it.

Again, we should think of verse 1 as the proper reaction when coming to the assembly of the saints. If you love to worship, you will love the place of worship, and attendance will be a blessing. The God you love is the God Whose house it is. We should visualize here another pilgrim saying, "It's time to go in," and our pilgrim in this Psalm jumps to his feet, smiles, and his heart fills with excitement. He is going into the House of the Lord!

O to God that his reaction was our reaction as we come to God's church. This response is the needed heart attitude – no begging necessary, nor any promise of some spectacular entertainment, just a heart that says I want to go worship my Lord.

Those who say you can be as close to the Lord out of church or worshiping in the woods would've gotten a frown from this pilgrim that would've reflected the frown of the Lord.

B. Entered

In verse 2 the pilgrim is so happy because he's within a few steps of Jerusalem's gates. He's joyous because he's too close not to make it now. It's as if he's pausing to think: "Praise God, we made it." "I'm here; I'll get to be part of all of this." Remember in Psalm 121 the pilgrim struggled with the fears that he might not even make it. Now he specifically mentions "*gates*", which speak of a great city and implies safety and oasis from the world.

In our day, we would do well to remember that it was said of the church, "*the gates of hell shall not prevail against it*" (Matthew 16:18). The Lord's intention for every local church is that it would be such an oasis where we can leave the world out and come and worship our Lord. Fortunately for us, we're no longer forced to go to Jerusalem, but just down the road to our local church. So as the pilgrim said here, "*let us go*" and enter in.

II. Security in the House of the Lord (v. 3-5)

A. Fortified

We've already seen that the House of the Lord is that place of security, that oasis. We also rejoice to see the word "*builded*" as that itself is amazing when so many others wanted it down! Inside the gates the city "*is compact*". The thought here is that the homes would be very close to each other to get as many people as possible inside the safety of the gates and walls.

The city, freshly built by David, would have been so impressive for the pilgrim from the country. He would never have seen anything like it. Of course, he would never have seen its like from the rural areas or small towns from where he came, but he would have never seen anything like it in Jerusalem or anywhere else. This picture shows great similarity to a new Christian who dives into the things of the Lord including worship. That new

Christian will likely tell you that he or she has never seen anything like it either. Hopefully, we feel the same way coming into God's presence, and can surely look forward with anticipation to the heavenly Jerusalem.

This pilgrim probably thought: "I had a lot of dangers out on the road, but I'm safe here." That is as it should be. Can't you see here why a pastor must ever work to keep a church straight doctrinally and in God's will. Every Christian deserves that place of safety as God intended it. Lovely Jerusalem had been built by great King David, and the Church has been built by the Greater David, Jesus, the King of Kings. King Jesus has given those of us He has bought with His Own Blood the local church. Jerusalem is filled with gorgeous palaces just as the local church should be filled with a gorgeous spirit. It's fair, as well, to apply this thought in private worship. We further anticipate the Heavenly Jerusalem with its "*many mansions.*"[5]

B. *Unified*

In verse 4 we see that more than the buildings themselves was the attitude of the people too. They were lovingly "*compact*". This idea is clear in the unity of the various tribes coming up together. Again, in this Pilgrim Psalm that emphasizes the public aspect even more than the private, they came in that great unity that is also the need of every local church. Don't misunderstand unity. There was unity, yet the distinction of the tribes remains. It was a case of some differences, yet unity.

This unity blossomed into a unified goal, the goal of giving thanks to the Lord and worshiping Him. Here's where we modern-day pilgrims could learn so much from our forebears. If we'd be unified on the same basis they were, we could dodge so much of the trouble prevalent in our churches today. We need their unity of purpose. We need to be all about giving thanks and worshiping our Lord. Do you want to see how transforming this unity was? These

---

[5] There is an emphasis on Jerusalem here (v. 2,3,6) that must not be missed.

tribes were not described as "of Israel", but "*of the Lord*". They were His now.

In verse 5 we see that the pilgrims came by David's palace while they were there. They purposely sought out "*thrones of judgment*" when they came. They instinctively knew that righteousness and holiness are close companions of worship. In fact, the Lord is not interested in your worship without it. That's why some of what passes for worship in our day just won't fly. When the companions of worship are run off, worship just won't stick around.

Further, justice and peace go together. David was a just King and he was exactly what Jerusalem needed. The word "*thrones*" is mentioned twice so that we would not fail to key in on justice. This emphasis is why a local church needs to conform to God's Word and things like church discipline are essential for a church to be a place where the Lord can be truly worshiped.

III. Peace in the House of the Lord (v. 6-9)

A. Praying

The words "*peace*" and "*prosper*" rise to prominence in the final verses of this Psalm. In that Jerusalem means "the city of peace", it comes as no surprise. Notice, too, that in verse 6b the Psalmist begins speaking directly and beautifully to Jerusalem and does so until the end of the Psalm.

"*They shall prosper that love thee*" –that is at once a promise and a threat. May all countries, including our own, heed that warning! Again, there's really a play on words here as we pray for "*peace*" for Jerusalem, the "city of peace." There's a prophetic element in this Psalm as it looks forward to the ultimate fulfillment of when the Prince of Peace returns. These pilgrims pray, in a sense, the same thing we New Testament Christians are to pray: "*even so, come, Lord Jesus.*"

The beautiful thing about this prayer is that all will profit from its peace. Peace here is more than the absence of war, but the presence of prosperity and happiness. In the same sense, the local church should have peace in the same fashion that was sought in Jerusalem. We can't help but notice, sadly, that Jerusalem didn't have peace in Jesus' day, nor even in our day, and many churches don't either.

When you see the word "*prosperity*", you are reminded that there are many Old Testament promises of prosperity. On the other hand, the New Testament focuses more on promised adversity as that pays better spiritual dividends and adds more to the net worth of life. In verse 7 the prayer is specifically that this peace be "*within thy walls*". That's the same desperate need of our churches today. And remember, as it becomes increasingly clear in this Psalm, if there is no peace, there is no worship. In addition, remember peace must always precede prosperity!

Logically, the Lord is inside Jerusalem's gates, so it's natural for her to have peace. If you believe that it's the same Lord Who gave us the local church, you should naturally surmise that there should be that same peace. In verse 8 it's suggested that we should be motivated for peace for the sake of our fellow pilgrims. We Christian pilgrims today can look at that Christian over on that other church bench and remember that he or she needs peace no matter how we feel about it. For the record, the local church is a place they should be able to get that peace, so we had better learn to be peaceful. Let us pray for peace in our local churches.

B. Serving

"*The house of the Lord*" in verse 9 ends this Psalm just as it began in verse 1. That there be no confusion, God's presence is the only reason Jerusalem is great. You see, God chose Jerusalem. In the same way, He chose to have the local church and work through it and its imperfect people. Though it may have troubles, if the Lord chose it, I'll seek all the good for it I can. Because God's presence is necessary for a place of worship, whether it be the Old Testament Temple or the New Testament church, I'll work toward it. "*Seek*" is a strong word. I'll make every effort to promote the local church and help it. This seeking will naturally mean service, and so we all have a work to do in the local church. Pilgrim, let's deal with this fact on our difficult pilgrimage until we can say from the depths of our hearts: *"Let us go into the house of the Lord."*

5

Until

Psalm 123

Just wait. Those aren't our favorite words, but they are often our most needed. This Psalm contains truths that the pilgrims heading to Jerusalem knew they needed. In equal measure, the Christian pilgrim needs to deal with these things as he or she marches into God's presence. There are some burdens on the soul that must be unloaded to properly worship the Lord. Amid troubles and problems, we must see that it isn't a question of "if" the Lord will deliver us, only a matter of *"until"*.

I. The Upward Look (v. 1)

A. *I Need Help*

The traveling pilgrims near the gates of Jerusalem. He will need lodgings, he must take steps to secure sacrifices, and he must make other arrangements before he goes to the Temple. That takes time and adds to whatever stress he may have already been dealing with. Here in this fourth Song of Degrees verse 1 begins as a solo as the pilgrim sings alone.[6] Notice the singular pronouns throughout.

---

[6] This Song of Degrees is actually the first Psalm in the second cycle. The cycles are three psalms each with five cycles total in the Pilgrim Psalms.

The Pilgrim has made progress in Psalm 121. In Psalm 121 he needed the hills to remind him to look up. Now the pilgrim has already learned to look up to the Lord. He has learned the only place to look for all the dimensions of help needed. Perhaps this time he can look up and view the Temple itself and just naturally think of his Lord.

He's doing much looking to the Lord. Notice *"eyes"* are mentioned three times in this Psalm. We have no idea what his problems are in this Psalm, but we do know where he's looking. The direction of his look is constant as the Lord is always an upward look. Again, this pilgrim has learned that it's no good to cast his eyes in any other direction. When we're in trouble, we had better remember that upward is the direction we must look. It isn't down at our problems, or our corrupt world, that we need to look, or we'll only fall deeper into despair. We'd better not look inward either as there are no answers there and that look would only lead to foolish pride or deceptive conclusions.

For the record, verse 1 is a great testimony for any believer to have. Christian pilgrim, we should always look beyond ourselves and upward to the Lord. We must be careful as the flesh always wants to look any direction except upward. That's why it took the hills in the previous Psalm to get us looking in the right direction. Looking up isn't pride – it's faith. If our faith was in ourselves, we would not have looked up at all. We look up because we need help.

B. He Can Help

This pilgrim addresses the Lord as *"O thou that dwellest in the heavens"*. *"Dwellest"* is a word of peace that references calm and control and points to His throne. *"Heavens"* speaks to the scope of His control reminding us that nothing can take away that peace, calm, and control. This calm and control are not confined to the Temple Mount in Jerusalem, or to our church, or even to the area where our problems exist, but to all.

This throne is an occupied throne that declares that God's universe is fully in His control. See, that's what reminds me to always look up, that leads to prayer, that leads to faith no matter the ugly, sad things around me. Again, I have the Lord, and I know what He is, Who He is, and where He is! Perhaps Israel hasn't lived up to the truth of this testimonial, but someday she will. We Christian pilgrims should live up to the glorious certainty of verse 1 every day.

II. The Waiting Look (v. 2)

A. I Will Watch

We see a distinct change in verse 2. The singular "I" gives way to the plural "*our*" and "*us*" the rest of the way. We hear the beauty of the choir as the soloist is joined by the lilt of many voices.

"*Behold, as*" is like saying "see how" as if these pilgrims are speaking to the Lord. Usually, it is the Lord Who says "*behold*" to us. Many opinions exist on the analogy of servants that is used here, but it's quite clear what is being addressed. On the one hand, in those days particularly servants of masters, or maidens who were servants for ladies, were trained to keep their eyes on their master at every moment. If the master was entertaining guests, the servant doesn't watch the guests at all, but keeps his or her eyes ever on the master to see what the master wants done next. "*Eyes*" call for full attention.

Such a complete attention speaks of obedience. The servants are waiting only for guidance, a guidance that will be obeyed immediately. Many Christian pilgrims can't use Psalm 123 for help, or can't live up to verse 1, because they have no intention of living up to what is said here in verse 2. Many in our day want help, and even in a way look to Him for that help, but they have no intention of practicing obedience on the way to the help. Don't mistake this analogy as approval for slavery as that is not being commented on here at all. The analogy is simply drawn from a life experience common in their day. The point, then, is that we are to be willing servants and always looking to our Master.

Additionally, when the "*hand of their masters*" is mentioned, it is about provision as servants in those days would have to look to the master for food, clothing, shelter, and medical care as they would have no means of their own at all. Pilgrim, from our Lord's hand, our Master, comes all our provision. This is true whether we believe it or not as we have absolutely no means of our own outside of the Lord. We submit to our Lord because we know that not only do we depend on Him, but beyond this servant analogy, He truly loves us. Yes, *"our eyes"* should always turn to look toward Him. From Him, we get all our guidance and provision. We have problems, pilgrim, and we know there's nowhere else to look but to the Master.

B. He Will Move

Our eyes *"wait upon the Lord our God"*. In other words, we are to stay focused on Him until He makes His move. *"Until"* is the word of this Psalm. It is the word for waiting. The only hope is waiting on the Lord. We must be looking to the future where our Lord will provide mercy. We think in terms of "if" He brings mercy, but faith says it's only *"until"*. His mercy is coming and the only issue that remains is the matter of timing.

Many follow verse 1 and the first half of verse 2 for a while, but still allow the comfort of this Psalm to slip from their grasp because they can't wait. We can wait because His help is sure. Looking back, do we not have many episodes from our journey where we have waited, perhaps not as patiently as this Psalmist, and yet help has always come?

Sometimes our troubles have stretched over years, but the Lord has never failed us. It may be true that our faith while waiting has wavered and caused us problems, but He has not failed us. *"Until"*– write it in big letters on your heart. Scream *"until"* loudly until you recapture your faith. Because of the God described in verse 1, we can wait *"until"*.

III. The Prayerful Look (v.3-4)

A. I Will Ask

In these last two verses, this Psalm becomes full of repetition because there are things we must not fail to learn. First, we notice that *"have mercy upon us"* is mentioned twice. *"Have mercy"* is asking the Lord to show favor and be gracious. The pilgrim is pleading for the only source of help. Although verse 2 says *"until"*, he still prays here for mercy. To ask the Lord for mercy is not claiming that we deserve anything, but only stating that we believe the fact that the Lord is merciful.

It is God's plan that we trust His *"until"*, but that we also continue to ask in prayer about it. No doubt, this continued prayer is to keep our faith active and strong. The lesson is to pray as you look upward and don't give up on *"until"*. We pilgrims, of course, don't understand waiting *"until"*, but the Lord has some great purpose. As we learned in verse 1, He sees from the throne.

B. He Will Be Waited Upon

As of yet, we have never heard in this Psalm what the pilgrim's problem is. In fact, we've only discussed the additional problems that have arisen from it. Clearly, this withholding of information to this point is so that you and I may apply it to any problem in our lives. This Psalm is still not going to tell us what the original problem was, but we are going to see that facing contempt developed inside the problem.

"Contempt" is mentioned twice and means ridicule or sarcasm and carries the idea of extreme arrogance or condescension. As we have already come to see, waiting *"until"* is a matter of strong faith, but that doesn't mean you'll enjoy contempt. The reason people use contempt or ridicule against us is because it's so effective. It tears us apart and is most hurtful. We can count on the fact that we will face contempt if we truly follow the Lord. People will say things like: "if your God is so great, why are you suffering like this?" Another will proclaim: "you're wasting your life". You may even hear: "there's more money in a lifestyle outside of all this Christian stuff". The list goes on and on. It's a heaviness to any pilgrim's heart.

Regarding this contempt, twice we are told that the pilgrims are *"exceedingly filled"*. That means they were saturated with contempt, or completely overwhelmed. It's like they're saying, we are fed up; we've had all we can take. To be sure, this level of being overwhelmed can hinder us from keeping our eyes on Him "*until*".

Fortunately, the Psalmist never mentions turning back on the Lord to relieve the contempt as being an option. These pilgrims are only explaining what a pain it's been. The repetition in the phrase "*our soul is exceedingly filled*" highlights the effect this being overwhelmed is having as they come to the Lord's presence to worship in Jerusalem. In other words, they're confessing that they need to unload it.

These pilgrims reference the "*scorning*". They are facing derision and mockery. Perhaps they said something like: "you must drive that old car" or while roaring with laughter, "following God sure is valuable". The pilgrim describes those doing the scorning as being "*at ease*". That refers to people living in self-indulgence, people who appear to have no big problems, and are not concerned about yours. They are know-it-alls who condescendingly speak and don't help your situation in any way. Sometimes, they're even other Christians with a fake spirituality.

In many cases, these people are unwittingly helping Satan deceive you. Here you are suffering, and they seem to suggest that they are following God and they don't have problems or drop the hint that they have money in the bank, or even insinuate that they know how to take care of themselves. Did you notice that this Psalm doesn't preach at these scorners? We are pilgrims heading to God's presence and that is not the point here. No, the point is that I don't need to be swallowed up by them. I need His presence.

The word "*contempt*" is repeated in verse 4 while "*of the proud*" is added. "*Proud*" speaks here of arrogance and is hard to swallow as we can all struggle with being looked down on by important people. Can you handle being looked down on by the wealthy, the worldly, the educated? Does their smirk hinder you from triumphantly proclaiming you're waiting "*until*"?

The Bible is full of warnings that we will hear such contempt and arrogance. Remember II Peter 3:4 says, "*And saying, Where is the promise of his coming? for since the fathers fell asleep, all things continue as they were from the beginning of the creation.*" Such mockery can potentially take our eyes off the Lord's "*until*" if not faced head on. Pilgrims must deal with it.

On the surface, this Psalm appears to end unresolved. But that's simply not the case. No, these pilgrims are saying we're going back to verse 1 *("unto thee I lift up mine eyes, O thou that dwellest in the heavens"*), and waiting "*until*". In the meantime, we are going to sing on our way to the Lord's presence and we're not going to let these hindrances stop us. In other words, we're going to keep our eyes on the Lord and His precious "*until*".

6

The Lord Who Was on Our Side

Psalm 124

What if? ...that's a game we often play, usually in a negative, destructive way. Answering the what-ifs panic us as we think of all that could have happened. In this Psalm, we pilgrims will ask the what-ifs in a positive way. We will do it in a way that will fill our hearts with praise and thanksgiving as we think on *"the Lord who was on our side"*.

I. If (v. 1-2)

A. The Lord with Israel

This Song of Degrees is ascribed to David and coincidentally the pilgrims sing it as they travel to the city of David and God's Holy Temple. It appears they are in Jerusalem now and likely going through purification to enter the Temple. This Psalm has only plural pronouns. That shows us that there are no solo parts in this song. We have the whole choir throughout the entirety of this Psalm as it's one that every follower of the Lord can truly sing. This Psalm required a great number because all can give thanksgiving to the Lord. In fact, we all have huge accounts of thanksgiving owed to our Lord.

Some bicker over the occasion of this Psalm as it is difficult to determine the exact event in David's life being discussed.[7] While we know the background of some of the Psalms and it greatly aids

---

[7] As with most of these Pilgrim Psalms, some argue that they are from Hezekiah's or Nehemiah's time. Those arguments are based on the flimsiest of evidence and we see no reason to discard the heading we find in this Psalm in our Bibles.

our study, this Psalm will not yield itself to the discovery of any precise situation that might rob believers of the universality of it.

Notice the great emotion in this choppy sentence that is blurted out from a full heart. Notice all the italicized words where the KJV translators try to give the sense of the uneven sentence. "*If*" rhetorically points us to the Lord. We also read "*now*", which is used in the idea of looking back to see what is now obvious. We don't know exactly when "*now*" was, but "*now*" can always apply.

Israel's history illustrates the point being made here, so much so that she can step up and testify. She has always been on the verge of destruction and the Lord has repeatedly intervened on her behalf. From her early days when Abraham was growing old without an heir, to her days of bondage in Egypt, to her facing enemies in Canaan, and even to her own sin, the Lord has intervened for her time and time again. So many other nations hated her and sought her destruction. If the Lord hadn't been on Israel's side, there's absolutely no way she could have survived to David's time. Even more, without the Lord on her side she certainly could not have survived to our days.

B. The Lord with Us

In this great emotion, the pilgrim, who in this case was David, repeats himself. Again, we have: "*if it had not been the Lord who was on our side*". Seek more in this phrase than mere historical accuracy or an academic understanding of how God has helped Israel, though that is true and primary. David is emotional not only because the Lord loves Israel, but more importantly, as being one of Israel, the Lord loved him too. This protection and help were personally touching to him. In other words, he personally experienced it. Christian pilgrim, we believers are God's heavenly people and this whole Psalm fits us as perfectly as it does Israel. Her story, in many ways, is really our story.

He mentions next "*when men rose up against us*". We can grasp the words "*against us*" as the world, the flesh, and the devil are always out to get us. This grotesque trifecta ever seeks to destroy

God's people. "*If*" all these enemies had not run into the Lord who was on our side, we would have been destroyed. "*If it had not been*" has a specific object. It doesn't say, if I hadn't served the Lord so well, or if I hadn't obeyed so well: no, it just says "*the Lord*". It's all just been His mercy.

It's a great scene here where we are looking over the years, and at our present problem, and seeing the Lord has delivered again as always. The text says, "*now may Israel say*". In a case of perfectly legitimate application, I can sincerely read it "now may Jimmy say". The help of this Psalm is already becoming transparent. It's clear for the situation where the Lord is on our side and men rise up against us. Can't you see how that's going to turn out pilgrim?

II. Then (v. 3-5)

A. The Enemy Is a Devouring Beast

Do you remember if-then statements from your school days? You know – if this, then this. The two "*if*'s" of verses 1 and 2 lead to three "then's" in verses 3 through 5. If not the Lord, "*then*" what we have in verse 3. Like a wild beast, the enemy had us (it appeared) swallowed. "*Quick*" in this usage means alive. In other words, it's saying we were swallowed alive, and it happened so quickly that we could do nothing about it. There was no way we could react and escape. It was beyond our strength and ability. You could forget the enemy slowly chewing you up, as you were taken here in one gulp. The pilgrims were helpless.

Do you, pilgrim, see this as our being held in the worst clutches, seized as Hell had us sinners swallowed up in our sin, helpless, and dead in that sin? If it had not been for our Jesus Christ Who died and shed His Own blood for us, the clutches of our sin will have pulled us into the pit. No wonder the word "*wrath*" is used as there is a burning anger that stands over our sin as well. All Christian pilgrims have lived this verse.

B. The Enemy Is a Drowning Torrent

Here we encounter two more *"then"* statements. Specifically, we have a raging stream such as we might find in a sudden flash flood. I remember my Daddy would not allow me to play beside our usually calm creek near our mountain home in a rainstorm as it would so easily change from a play place to a raging torrent that could take your life. Obeying him was easy as I was afraid and wouldn't get too close when it roared from massive volumes of water. In the Smoky Mountains where I grew up, it would sometimes come a cloudburst on the high mountains that would rapidly come down the narrow hollows. My grandfather even told me of extreme cases where a wall of water would come down the river. I also remember seeing an old black-and-white picture of a man standing where his house stood just 20 minutes before. Once I also came around the corner on the Alum Bluff Cave Trail in the Great Smoky Mountains National Park and saw the landscape completely changed from my last hike by a flash flood. Israel had similar landscape that lended itself to these terrifying flash floods.

These waters were called *"proud"* to suggest that they appeared arrogant. These waters have an arrogant aura because we are so powerless when we are before them. These streams in this Psalm represent the great problems we have faced where we were so helpless. We are no more a match for the problems thrown at us by the world, the flesh, and the devil than if we were standing on the edge of a stream in a flash flood. Sometimes, too, we find the things that we thought would sustain us (outside of God) being washed away. In some cases, it's our money, our health, our friends, or our family that we see disappearing downstream. We thought we would be washed away with those things, but the Lord was on our side. Notice that the waters have their raging limited to <u>before</u> the Lord makes His move.

III. Escape (v. 6-8)

A. The Snare Is Broken

We see the metaphor changing from flood to fangs and fowler's snare to pile one graphic picture upon another. To keep the shocking picture in context, we read, *"Blessed be the Lord"*. We are trending to praise and thanksgiving. All the could-have-been's not coming to pass as we feared must lead us to praise. The pilgrim couldn't get on to the trapped bird example without stopping to offer thanksgiving to the Lord. We, too, should stop and thank Him often for His deliverances. Someone (the Lord) was there for us, and on our side, and didn't allow the enemies that were far more powerful than us to overtake us. What can't be denied is that the Lord likes to do this for us!

Notice that the word *"snare"* is used twice. We were as helpless as caught prey and the Lord yanked us out before the teeth crushed us. We truly are like an escaped bird. Have you ever watched a trapped bird, or even a wilder chicken that is cornered, and see their absolute terror and panic? Just like us, a bird is so fragile compared to those who would hurt them. This pilgrim didn't see that he was walking into a trap until it caught him.

Often a trap is set with something that would attract the bird, like food. We are often likewise entrapped. Though we were not told the type of bird trap used here, we can certainly rehearse the traps used on us. George Barlow says the bait of worldliness, selfishness, and unbelief are laid out and then we're caught.

We were caught, ensnared, and backed into a corner where the Lord moved and released us. There's no thrill quite like the thrill of escape. For the two mentions of *"snare"* the Lord has given us two mentions of *"escaped"*. The snare was set, but because of the Lord's intervention the snare is like a broken net that lost its power to trap. No trap can hold us when the Lord decides to break it. Perhaps you can remember episodes of being trapped in your life and can look back today realizing the Lord delivered you. Escape! Escape, yes, because of *"the Lord who was on our side"*.

We pilgrims should think again of our sin, and the judgment we faced in the flames, and remember that the Lord sent us His gospel and let us escape. That escape more than anything proves He is *"the Lord who was on our side"*.

B. The Lord Is Our Help

"Our help is in the name of the Lord". There's no other name rather than *"the Lord"* Who could provide such daring escapes. Look at verse 1 again: *"if it had not been the Lord who is on our side, now may Israel say"*. We end where we began – with the Lord. For the believing Pilgrim, this is always so! He is the One we call on and from Whom we have received help from. Don't let the word *"help"* escape your notice as we are so needy and helpless.

Now we are escaped and can thank God for what we have been delivered from. All the graphic language of this Psalm shows how completely overwhelmed we were, and yet we escaped! For pilgrims like us, it's salvation and 1000 things more.

He is the Lord *"who made heaven and earth"*. Look up at the heavens, and round at the earth, and think of the strength of God and how He has delivered you. Pilgrim, you can believe Him and have faith because He is *"the Lord who was on our side"*. Remember Romans 8:31 says, *"What shall we then say to these things? If God be for us, who can be against us?"* Remember, pilgrim, it's not who's against us that matters, but Who that is on our side. Praise His Name, He is *"the Lord who was on our side"*.

7

As Mount Zion

Psalm 125

Do you ever get confused about what will last and what will pass away? What things are eternal and what things are for a time only? The cares of life, if focused on, will weaken our faith, and make us imagine a reversal in our minds of two antagonists that are known as the eternal and the temporal. The Pilgrim traveling up to the presence of God must trust in the Eternal Lord Who makes us *"as Mount Zion"*.

I. What Is Eternal (v. 1-2)

A. The Value of Trusting the Lord

We meet here another Song of Degrees whose background is unknown to us, though they all seem to be from the time of David or Solomon. As this Psalm goes along it refers to being under the rod of an oppressor. This fact intensifies the speculation of the historical setting, but it's a reflection on all of Israel's history. Do we not remember Egypt? Do we not remember the oppressive cycle that Israel repeated in the time of the Judges? As with so many of these Psalms, the background is obscured so that the application might be timeless. We find no soloists in this song as the choir sings every word. This song demands this arrangement as this Psalm is for all of God's pilgrims always.

We can visualize pilgrims crossing the hills of Jerusalem and seeing the Temple before them. As you can imagine, that would call for a song for these weary pilgrims. They've already learned the lesson of Psalm 121:1, the lesson of *"I will lift up mine eyes unto the hills, from whence cometh my help"*. The Pilgrim is probably thinking about how insecure life is, as well as how tottering the world is. But as he tops the hill and sees Mount Zion, he thinks of the Lord and His comfort, and he remembers to trust. Though the pilgrim makes no mention of the Temple this time as the buildings of Mount Zion have come and gone, that mountain remains.

"They that trust in the Lord" is a description the pilgrim hopes rings true for himself. For that category of person, it says here that they shall be *"as Mount Zion"*. In other words, if we have trust in our Lord we shall be *"as Mount Zion"*, which is stable, unchanging, and eternal. No analogy could ever be more encouraging to a Hebrew than that of Mount Zion. Though many things are open to destruction, they all know that Mount Zion shall never be removed.

Were we to miss the words *"in the Lord"* we would undermine the entire verse as that is the key to trust. In the first instance, we see here the eternal life that we receive when we put our trust in Jesus Christ and were saved, but it goes much further. The pilgrim here has no doubt, or lack of trust, that the Lord was the God of Israel and that he as an individual was one of God's own. No, the place where trust is a strain is in living faith, the task of trusting the Lord amidst a topsy-turvy world. Christian pilgrim, if we can have a real, vibrant, living faith in our Lord every day, and in every situation, we can be stable *"as Mount Zion"* in our scary world.

At times, the Temple was destroyed, but Mount Zion remains. Like Mount Zion, some of the buildings that we have erected in our lives come and go, but the mountain remains. We speak of seeing what is eternal and it's our Lord Whom we trust Who stands beyond time. For that reason, what we do about Him is all that remains, or *"abideth forever"*. The Lord, Who is eternal, stands above all the naughty movers and shakers whose power is clearly locked inside time and can't touch the eternal.

B. The Value of His Protection

No matter which ridge you top to reach Jerusalem, you will see you are part of a circle of hills around Jerusalem. *"Round about"* is mentioned twice to emphasize the surrounding hills. In ancient warfare, the surrounding hills would be an invaluable protection. As mountainous around Jerusalem, so *"the LORD"* surrounds us. Jehovah is also mentioned twice in the first two verses to highlight what surrounds us. The Lord is better than mountains as He is even the Rock that holds up the mountains.

"His people" in verse 2 is tied to *"they that trust"* in verse 1. Again, we see that our eternal life is held up by Him Who could say *"neither shall any man pluck them out of my hand"* (John 10:28). Beyond that, our Lord is a daily hedge for us, as he was for Job. That hedge is ever protecting us amid our difficult days. Many of us don't worry about the Lord allowing us to slip out of His hand, and lose our eternal life, but our struggle is the looming problems in our home, health, work, or family where we forget that He is the hedge that surrounds us as the hills surround Jerusalem.

Yes, the troubled pilgrim of this Psalm should sing of the Lord's protection as he walks along to God's presence. Enemies must get by Jerusalem's mountain to get to her, and so to get to us, our enemies must get around our Lord. If you don't believe this is true, just ask Satan. In his efforts to get Job, he saw the reality of how strong the hedge that's erected by our Lord really is.

II. What Is Not (v. 3)

A. The Work of Chastening

Despite all that was said about Mount Zion, her history records that enemies walked her ridges. Several times Jerusalem has been conquered by enemies. The point is not that enemies could never touch her, but that her conquering has never been eternal. She bounces back after her conquerors have passed off the scene. Our own history as modern-day pilgrims is the same. This Psalm will now trace out the difference between chastening and permanent judgment.

"The rod" is mentioned. Though some point out that the word *"rod"* can mean "scepter or rule", which appears to be true when Jerusalem fell under the rule of these invaders, the word can also refer to discipline. Clearly, discipline of God's people is in view here. These armies didn't slip through God's fingers, nor did they trample under foot His hedge, but they were sent through by the Lord for the good of His people. Even under the rod, pilgrim, you are in His care.

When the text says, *"shall not rest upon the lot the righteous"*, we are reminded that the rod won't stay. The rod only visits! It's not eternal and won't last forever as in the case of His enemies. Satan's big lie is that the rod is permanent. Remember that no matter how severe the rod, Jerusalem has always arisen from the ashes. In the same manner, so it is with us in Jesus Christ. Further, the Lord gets Jerusalem as His earthly throne site someday and we pilgrims of His will be in that Kingdom. We must learn to distinguish our eternal destination from the bumpy roads of time.

B. The Thought of Despair

Again, the rod does not stay *"upon the lot of the righteous"*. We may be under the rod for a while, but if we trust, it will never push us to despair and on into sin. Correction yes; destruction no. Thomas Adams said, "unless heaven could lose God, we cannot lose heaven". No one will ever permanently take Jerusalem, or for that matter, any of the Lord's pilgrims.

The phrase *"lest the righteous put forth their hands unto iniquity"* demonstrates that the rod is only for correction. Correction is not to destroy you, but to help you with the future. The Lord loves His pilgrims, and He knows what we've done and what we need. On that basis, He carefully sends the rod. The rod of chastening may be painful in the short term, but the pilgrim can rest assured that it will never go as far as the rod of judgment.

III. An Eternal Principle Working in Time

A. Pray the Promises

Verse 4 begins a prayer that will finish out this Psalm. When the pilgrim prays, "*do good, O Lord*", he asks the only One Who is "*good*" or Who can do good. We must all seek the Lord for "*good*" as the only good any of us can hope for is to be made good by Christ. As it turns out, the usage of the word "*good*" does not refer here to the theological sense of being saved but is used in the wider sense of doing better or being cheered.

"*Good*", then, is a reference to the "*good*" thing being asked of us in this Psalm: "*trust in the Lord*" (verse 1). Let us trust Him so that our Lord can cheer us even if still under that rod. We are, in effect, praying the promises because that reminder increases faith in a time where it's most needed.

B. The Depth of the Rod

Most leave the sense of this Psalm to interpret this verse and so teach wrongly. You can read opinions across the spectrum-- everything from losing your salvation to being a false professor. The problem is that this Psalm is about the rod of correction for God's own, not the rod of judgment against nonbelievers. This Psalm is explaining what sin can do to us and what the Lord must do about it. But with that knowledge of sin, we should see how it's possible in the Lord to be "*as Mount Zion*" instead of living the unstable life that characterizes so many believing pilgrims.

The phrase "*as for such as turn aside*" is only one word in the Hebrew language, which means to bend away, and is usually, as here, used in a moral sense. Still, the word is not exclusive to nonbelievers. If we don't respond to the Lord in our problems or when under the rod, we might turn to "*crooked ways*". The crooked way is far more difficult than the straight path. This is a warning to all pilgrims. At this point, especially, the Lord must activate the rod. That is, of course, detrimental to a pilgrim seeking the Lord's presence.

When it says that the Lord *"shall lead them forth"*, which is another phrase that is one word in Hebrew, it is meant in the same sense as in Psalm 23:4 where the Shepherd leads in our lives. Our Lord is leading us where we need to go. He even leads us where we need to go when we are on *"crooked ways"*. That trail might go by the rod of correction. Don't let the phrase *"with the workers of iniquity"* confuse you. It says, *"with the workers of iniquity"*, not "as the workers of iniquity". There's a world of difference in those two phrases.

"The workers of iniquity" are the unsaved and the pilgrims in this Psalm are going along with them. The point is simple: the rod of chastening can resemble the rod of judgment. Remember the Corinthian Christians who got sick and died because of their carnality? But the similarities end there! One path ends in Heaven and the other in Hell! It is only here in time where the two paths resemble. In these times of chastening the pilgrim may not appear to be the Lord's, but he still is. The effects of chastening may weary a pilgrim traveling to the presence of the Lord, but he or she must unload those hard feelings while seeing the loving work of the Lord.

The Psalm finishes with *"but peace shall be upon Israel"*. The pilgrim will not be left hanging in the negative, so the positive is brought out to send us back to verse 1 to *"trust in the Lord."* As we go back to trusting the Lord, let us remember that we should always trust under the rod, and perhaps not need further work with the rod that can so resemble judgment. That *"peace"* is what every pilgrim desperately needs. What is this *"peace"*? It's the peace of God's protection, the peace of knowing what's eternal and what is not, the peace of which the pilgrim gladly sings, and, yes, it's a peace in our unstable world of being in Christ *"as Mount Zion"*.

8

Like Them That Dream

Psalm 126

Have you ever been happy? Have you ever experienced real joy? Has it been a long time? Do you ever look back to a time when you were happy, or had real joy, like that joy you had when you first received Christ? Do you ever get burdened down wondering what happened to that joy? That loss is something that will bog you down in your Christian pilgrimage. It will affect you on the way to the presence of the Lord if you look back to the good, old days as one "*like them that dream*".

I. A Dream That Was Real (v. 1-2)

A. Help Given

As with several others, the events of this Pilgrim Psalm aren't told. Several scholars have equated it to the Babylonian captivity, but all these Pilgrim Psalms seem to be more of David's time. For the record, the word "*captivity*" that is used here could refer to any crisis. The city of Jerusalem was at war or even besieged, and had the problems as described in this Psalm, on many occasions.

The "*captivity of Zion*" mentioned here refers to Jerusalem, which was both the place that Psalm 125 told us could not "be removed" and the destination of these pilgrims. Times of war or being besieged would keep these traveling pilgrims away at certain times. Such a hindrance in getting to the presence of the Lord would certainly be heartbreaking. The end of such times of combat and trouble would be hoped for until it came and celebrated when it did.

In the first part of this Psalm, the pilgrim reflects on an amazing, spectacular episode *"when the Lord turned again the captivity of Zion"*. *"Turned again"* refers to being restored. You can tell as you read this Psalm that it must have been a supernatural intervention where things looked hopeless and then the Lord stepped in. This intervention brought on such euphoria among the pilgrims that they were *"like them that dream"*.

Perhaps you can visualize this extraordinary scene. Perhaps you have seen video footage of people delivered. Or better yet, perhaps you can look back and remember when Christ intervened into your broken, sinful life and you passed from death to life. Can you remember that euphoria in your soul? Beyond your salvation, perhaps you remember other deliverances the Lord gave you during your Christian pilgrimage. Many have been delivered from the bondage of drunkenness, hatred, or a host of other sins. Others have seen a health crisis, or some other major problem resolved by the Lord when all seemed hopeless. Sometimes the Lord steps in and so blesses and acts in our lives that we are *"like them that dream"*.

B. Joy Came

Imagine the scene as the word got to these pilgrims that the captivity, whatever it was, suddenly ended. People would say, "We can head back to Jerusalem! We can head back to God's presence!" It would be so tempting to pinch yourself and ask, "Am I dreaming?"

"Then" in verse 2 we have the turning point that suddenly brought on the celebration. This extraordinary event brought out laughter and giddiness. Both the *"mouth"* for laughing and the *"tongue"* for singing are mentioned. Apparently, the pilgrims were chattering 100 miles an hour about it. The pilgrims even burst out in song. It's like that scene where David slew Goliath. Can you imagine the incredible happiness in that crowd that sang, *"Saul hath

slain his thousands, and David his ten thousands"? The crowds melted into a great chorus in that episode.

In more recent times, it would be like our V-E and V-J days when the hostilities of World War II came to an end. Papers read: "War is over!" Tickertape parades filled the streets. Yes, it's easy to sing at these times. The Lord does such "*great things for them*" that are so unmistakably Him that even the unsaved attribute it to our Lord. What the Lord has done, especially in our salvation, and in these episodes of spectacular deliverance make for some of our greatest moments of happiness. Those moments are pure giddiness.

II. A Prayer That Is Needed (v. 3-4)

A. Help Remembered

Verse 3 begins a transition that confuses many readers. The pilgrims repeat: "*the Lord hath done great things for us*". The only difference is a change from "*them*" to "*us*", which is a confession where the pilgrims think, well, the heathen were right on that one! The difference is that where they say, "*for them*", we can say "*for us*". That is a world of difference.

Others can say it, these pilgrims can say it, but so can you and I say it Christian pilgrim. He has done great things for us. He has saved us through the blood of Jesus Christ! His salvation is the foundation of joy if you and I can keep our heads on straight and remember it. He's given us many other helps as well. Let's pause and remember. Deliverance, trouble fixed, victory when defeat seem sure – these glorious helps are the true story of our Christian lives.

B. Joy Requested

Now verse 1 where we had such an awesome experience is flipped to the prayer "*turn again our captivity, O Lord*". What's going on? Were verses 1 and 2 a dream? No. Do we still have access to Jerusalem pilgrim? Yes! We were "*glad*" in verse 3 but praying here to be restored or delivered again. Apparently, the laughter has died down. It always does. Euphoria has a short shelf life even if we still have the victory in hand. Many Christians still have the Lord in salvation, but the laughter is gone. The gladness gave way to frowns, and the great happiness we had is now a dull, joyless, even depression-filled journey. The experience of verses 1 and 2 grows so much fainter that we are even asking ourselves, "was it just a dream?"

Where it reads *"as the streams in the south"*, it refers to the southernmost area of Judah in the desert-like Negev. That area gets so dry as it receives rain only about one month out of the year. That is quite the dryness! With victory in hand, the pilgrims have still become dry. Even today, we are often dry and need that rain to get the streams of joy flowing again. Have you ever felt that way?

III. A Promise That Is No Dream (v. 5-6)

A. Help Assured

When you read verse 5 doesn't it seem so random, so completely out of the blue? Don't you want to scratch your head and ask what has it to do with our discussion? Don't miss it. It's one of the greatest of promises. It tells us something about life, particularly life in Christ, that we get so wrong. What is that apparently elusive promise? Happiness may come in euphoric moments, but joy can come even when there's tears. With that thought in hand, read again verse five: *"they that sow in tears shall reap in joy"*.

Joy may seem so far away that the pilgrim can encourage his heart as he goes to God's presence, maybe he's even reduced to tears. We shoot for more than fleeting happiness here and go for deep, abiding joy. Sowing and reaping are much used metaphors in the Bible. In the Christian life, the most common explanation is that the seed to be sown is the Word of God. Even Jesus beautifully uses it in that context; for example, in the parables of Matthew 13. Somehow that sowing is the clue for where joy really comes from.

As has often been preached, many take this verse as an application for sowing the Word of God to the lost and seeing them saved. That's a fair application, but the context is the problem the pilgrim has in his own heart. He needs to sow again that Word in his own life. He needs that deep interaction with God's Word that begets a closeness with the God Whose Word it is!

See the promise? Sow, even in your tears, and you will reap joy. This promise of sowing in tears and reaping in joy is a principal that carries a certainty of response and is one of the most untapped treasures of God's people. God is awesome! Only He could or would trade tears for joy. You sow, and as always, the Lord gives the increase, which in this case is joy. You don't need another euphoric experience to be happy. You need to sow the Word of God into your life till it springs into joy in your life again.

B. Joy Guaranteed

It seems verse 5 almost restates verse 4 in personal terms for double emphasis. Don't lose heart in barren, fruitless, unhappy times – just sow the Word of God into your life. Joy may seem too far away to ever reach, but the Word sown into your life will grow into the plant of abiding joy. Remember that season of David's life where he ran from Saul. He faced relentless pursuit from Saul, was ever on the run, and often had to hide out. Those were barren, unhappy days, yet he went on to real joy by sowing God's Word in himself until that accompanying closeness to the Lord yielded its peaceable fruit. This Psalm encourages all pilgrims to follow David's example.

It's strange that we had laughter in gladness in verses 1-3 while we have tears in verses 5-6. Still, we are much better off as this Psalm closes than we were when it began. This inverted dichotomy is one of the greatest examples of appearances being deceiving.

We're told that he "*goeth forth*". We pilgrims should read that and decide to keep going. It also said he goes as one who "*weepeth*". Don't buy the twisted version of Christianity that's often peddled in our day because, as the Psalmist says here, there will still be tears, hard times, and periods of parched earth in our pilgrim journey. Even if it's only through tear-dimmed eyes that see only failure instead of the path ahead, keep going Pilgrim! As the New

Testament says in Galatians 6:9, "*And let us not be weary in well doing: for in due season we shall reap, if we faint not.*"

Though the Psalmist goes weeping, notice what he carries: "*precious seed*". The seed is so great that we should just trust it. When it says, "*doubtless*", it speaks of a guarantee. When you sow God's Word, you reap joy. Remember, reaping only comes to sowers. No wonder there so many joyless Christians today – we don't sow!

When it speaks of "*sheaves*", it refers to good reaping, something substantial. No wonder that language is used as we speak of big stuff here; this promise is one of the big ones. And before you allow the tears to discourage you, notice the word "*rejoicing*". Despite it all, rejoicing is the ultimate lot of Christian pilgrims.

Tears are not forever to God's people. The Lord ever works to transform us and to take us from tears to rejoicing. That is really a double promise. There will be some rejoicing here to pilgrims who follow what this Psalm teaches, but much more in Heaven. For the record, too, the final rejoicing will far exceed the euphoria of the opening dreams. For one thing, it's a deeper experience

Pilgrim going to Jerusalem, or Christian going to God's presence, you must deal with your confusion of happiness for joy. Euphoria cannot exceed deep, abiding joy no more than the tears can exceed the ultimate rejoicing. We must deal with this as we go up to God's presence. Then, go on, pilgrim, and sow God's Word into your life. Just do it! Dreams in Christ do come true! There's far more for us than just to be "*like them that dream*".

9

Labor in Vain

Psalm 127

"I'm trying to get ahead", someone says. "I'm working my fingers to the bones", says another. "It's almost impossible to have a family in these hard times", and on and on. Most everyone wants to get ahead and be successful. Could it be that life's best blessings are under our noses while the treasures we seek are little more than junk? Could it be that our busy lives are only *"labor in vain"*?

I. The Divine Necessities (v. 1)

  A. Unbuilt Houses

No doubt the pilgrim marching to Zion may be wondering how to get ahead, or at least how to manage all the needs of his family. Maybe we all know something of the sleepless nights wondering if we can hold it all together. From those kinds of troubled thoughts springs this glorious Pilgrim song, a song on the things that desperately need attention as we travel to the presence of the Lord.

This Psalm is labeled "*a song of degrees for Solomon*". Some argue that it should read "by Solomon", or is about Solomon's Temple, but would it not be logical for David to first address these issues to Solomon? To my mind, it's natural to date this with those of David's time.

The Psalm opens with "*except the Lord*". The word "*except*" means "unless", and as this phrase is mentioned twice, it's a key to understanding the beginning of this Psalm. The thought is that we must depend upon the Lord completely. Naturally, a pilgrim will think of his home. The idea is the big picture of our home that includes the necessity of making a living. In that sense, our career is in view as well. Can we all admit that our homes, and especially the provision needed to sustain our homes, can be some of the great stressors in life? This Pilgrim Psalm suggests that our worry is wasted stress because all depends on the LORD Jehovah. No matter the house – your home, their Temple, our church – we need the Lord.

A phrase that captures in miniature so much of our lives given here is "*labor in vain*". The word "*vain*" is mentioned three times and is a keyword to pull our minds the direction they need to go. The word means "empty" and carries the idea of useless or meaningless. Further, don't blur the word "*labor*" here either. "*Labor*" usually has good connotations in Scripture. The Lord often explains that hard work is good for us. For the record, you must work at building your home, just don't think that you make it happen, or that good results are from your hands only.

To capture the meaning here we should ask ourselves the question, is getting the home built all that matters? That thinking is why some become swallowed up in their careers. Is building your home all that matters? The bigger and more impressive the better? Don't you even see it must be blessed by the Lord to be anything? To borrow another biblical analogy, no matter how grand your building, your foundation is sand without the Lord. How many apparently successful homes (or even churches) look so beautiful yet are already collapsing with its occupants already subjected to elements not even noticed.

B. Unkept Cities

The role of the watchman was a vital one in cities in those days. People put their trust in the watchman and any dereliction of duty on the watchman's part is devastating to everyone. Despite that dependence on watchmen, people could begin drawing the wrong conclusions. How quickly we forget that it's the Lord Who keeps the city, not the watchmen. The context of this whole Psalm is your home including your family, so the city is just another reference to it even if it seems to speak of Jerusalem, though the truth of it would apply there too as there are clear parallels. Watchmen, do your duty as the Lord commands, but never misunderstand Who keeps the city. You may be the watchman (don't forget that), but you desperately need the Lord.

Although cities like Jerusalem have watchmen and great walls, they've found out they are not invincible as the Lord's hand is the true protection. When things are going well we get overconfident and read too much into our efforts, but then in trouble the house collapses. Who knows what will happen in your home or city. It may be attacked, or reduced to ashes in a fire, or you may die in it, before you even have the chance to enjoy it. Some have impressive-looking walls that couldn't even hold off a gentle breeze. Some have $200,000 homes that are but rubble. They are houses that don't resemble a home. We need clearer perception here.

II. The Wasted Labor (v. 2)

A. Losing Time

The picture drawn here is of one getting up early, staying up late, and giving it their all. You scheme, fret, study, and plan, all to get ahead. Think about those worries the pilgrim carries about his home and remember that even dedication to your work, though commendable, will not alone pull it off. Just working harder alone won't make it better because we need the Lord. In many cases, we aren't even accomplishing what we think we are.

The phrase *"the bread of sorrows"* refers to earning our wages or getting financial gain. In fact, the word *"sorrows"* refers to toil. That's the difficult toil that goes all the way back to Adam. Though the Bible clearly commands us to provide for our families, the thought here is that the worry and overly focusing on financial gain aren't getting us anywhere. We are failing to see the real needs. For example, the extra money earned on overtime may cost you two or three times as much in your family! Warped priorities can overthrow expected results. Such examples are an unusual case of wasting time by doing more.

B. Losing Sleep

The Bible commends early rising and not oversleeping, but that's not the point here. The emphasis in this case is on our fretting about getting ahead. When we trust the Lord, our nights are not filled with sleeplessness, but as it says here, *"he giveth his beloved sleep"*. Trust Him! That brings rest as He gives peaceful sleep. Don't lay awake fretting and scheming about how to make things go. I imagine many of us pilgrims have done this far too many times. I know I have! And it did me no good.

Pilgrims traveling to Jerusalem probably spent much time as they lay down to sleep on the trail worrying about their families. Modern-day pilgrims lie in the bed anxious about many family issues too. Maybe it's eyes wide open in the darkness thinking of a coworker who got the promotion instead of you, or maybe you're lying there horrified that your investment portfolio lost 3%. The possibilities are endless.

Remember envy, bitterness, and anxiety won't build the things that you need building in your life. There's no provision for you or yours there. In fact, pilgrim, unload them. Have you ever noticed how these things that we get so stressed out over are things that the Lord isn't even concerned about? These sleepless nights are of our own creation as we are pursuing the wrong direction. This viewpoint here is not to suggest being lazy, but that we work in love for duty rather than for success holding to the larger context of the Lord's provision.

II. The Real Treasure (v. 3-5)

A. A Valuable Heritage

While verse 3 appears to start a new subject, that is not really the case at all. We've been seeing that we have often given our labor to the wrong things, with the effect that we "*labor in vain*", but now we're being turned back toward what is valuable. Perhaps we've misunderstood completely. Perhaps what we claim is for our beloved family was in fact selfish reasons. Because of those misunderstandings, the Lord is going to explain what labor <u>not</u> in vain is. When we finally see it, we will see that our aim should have been for the eternal all along.

"*Children*" are mentioned twice so that we will see the point we should have seen all along. We labor for treasure for our children, but our children are the treasure. The things we think we earned through overwork or successful scheming can never match the riches of the children themselves.

These children are called "*an heritage*". The idea of that word is that it is something inherited. Funny, I thought the children inherited from the parents, but here it's the other way around. Our children are an undeserved inheritance from the Lord. Further, the idea of the word is something that is an heirloom. Think of how you view and treat an heirloom. Do you not handle heirlooms carefully, cautiously, and with love and respect?

This heritage, or heirloom, also carries the connotation of something that is yours permanently. Do you see why money can never be called an heirloom? A heritage is to be valued and lived within. It gives a definition to life as something to inherit and pass on. Add godliness to it and it's of incredible value. Your heritage is not "*labor in vain*".

Heritage. Can't you see it? It's not our brilliant scheming, but a stewardship. We so often give our strength to the wrong things; for example, the company over the kids, and so we fail and *"labor in vain"*. It's so meaningless. Children not distinctly raised for the Lord are a wasted heritage. It's time we drop the futile rationalizations and finally see our children as the gift from God they are.

Further, the word *"reward"* doesn't match the outlook of many pilgrims. If it's a reward, it's not a burden. Do you see how children from the Lord gain you all you attempted to gain by scheming? A reward! Children are a reward and a blessing, not a mistake, or an accident, or a nuisance. It's most bizarre to call your blessings a nuisance.

We must come to learn that it's the Lord Who builds a home; we just follow Him. Don't panic about your finances but enjoy your heritage and reward. Those children are the thing that has the greatest potential to enrich your life if you just approach it properly. If your goal in life is just to leave a big inheritance to your children, you missed it. Those children are the inheritance and family is God's greatest gift outside of salvation. We pilgrims need our heads on straight.

B. A Full Quiver

The last two verses of this Psalm illustrate how children are an example of how the Lord strengthens your life and gives you what your scheming and fretting could never produce. Though we rarely think of it that way, it's time we did.

Children can protect and help you in your times of special weakness. Most lives will have times of such weakness whether it be in sickness or old age. Here the Lord allegorizes children as *"arrows"*. The idea is that children raised for God and cherished as an heirloom will stand together with you in a fight because banded together by love. That they were a treasure becomes obvious as we all value security. For the record, that's security that riches can never give you. The investment portfolio of your children far exceeds anything your banker or stockbroker can put together. In other words, that's quite a return on investment (ROI) in children! People in a selfish and self-satisfied life miss this reality, but if they live long enough it will likely become apparent. We pilgrims on our way to the presence of the Lord shouldn't wait but change our outlooks now.

Using arrows to draw this picture, several aspects about children become obvious. The worse the battle, the more arrows you'll need. When you think about it, remember we don't really know the future. This does not mean that we pilgrims are required to have all the children we biologically could have, but that we should seek the Lord as He always guides seeking pilgrims about their needs.

Though we speak of heritage, heirlooms, and treasure, we don't deny these arrows are work. Arrows must be worked out from rough, knobby branches. It takes work to treat them as the blessing they are, but it's encouraging to know that our work is not "*labor in vain*". Our work is to handle them as an heirloom and mold them from a branch to a godly arrow. As Henry Smith, who lived in the 1500s, said, "well doth David call children 'arrows' for if they are well bred, they shoot at their parent's enemies; and if evil bread, they shoot at their parents". Which way do your arrows fly, pilgrim?

Verse 5 begins with "*happy is the man*". The word "*happy*" means content. In other words, we're talking about God's way to real contentment. The Psalmist speaks of the full "*quiver*". A quiver holds our weapons. We all want weapons at hand when the battle is difficult and are glad that the quiver is accessible and full at such a time. When they're children or babies we protect them, but finally these blessings protect us. It's an understanding every pilgrim needs.

Sadly, this lesson is too often wasted. Even the wise Solomon allowed this lesson to get past him. A heritage must be protected and passed on to retain value. Anything less, and we've trashed our heritage. An heirloom that is valuable in only one generation is not much of an heirloom. Solomon wrote much on vanity and emptiness, and then by failing to grasp the truth about his children being a heritage, he experienced the vanity and emptiness he wrote about himself. Isn't the work that demands our greatest efforts becoming clearer?

When we read *"they shall not be ashamed "*, we see the results that God's way of raising children provides. If our children have become an embarrassment to us, we clearly are not doing it the way the Lord intended. Perhaps we were careless in the molding of our arrows. This is not a guarantee that our children will never stray or have problems, but a proclamation that they will be a blessing to us.

Notice *"but they shall speak with the enemies in the gate"*. Remember in Bible times that legal transactions took place at the city gate. The idea here is that when enemies try through legal maneuvers to attack us, our children will gladly speak up for us. This statement suggests that no matter the type of battle, our arrows will be ready.

The text said happy is such a man. Do you feel that way, pilgrim? I do. Despite the brokenness in my own life, I wouldn't trade my six treasures for Bill Gates wealth! Remember how the Psalm opened with *"except the Lord"*? What kind of house would it be any way if it couldn't be passed on forever? A word to those pilgrims who've not been blessed with children--pour your heart into other's children and reap the principle of this promise.

Pilgrim, have you been fretting about your family? Have you been obsessed with your finances to provide for your family? Is it hindering you as you travel to the presence of the Lord whether in private or in public worship? It's time to cast off that hindrance. Pilgrim, marching to God's presence, as you sing in your journey, look around and notice those little ones playing at your feet, and see that there goes your treasure and reward. As you look, rejoice that it's the opposite of *"labor in vain"*.

Gut check time! Perhaps you read this and though you agree it is the ideal, that ideal now seems out of your grasp. Perhaps the damage is already done. Perhaps your children are grown or any one of a host of other possibilities. Perhaps like me, you look at your family and must admit some brokenness, some caused by me, and some caused by others. Encourage your heart as I do mine in that the Lord didn't provide this psalm only for those who got it all right. We are traveling pilgrims all with our own unique journey. We are obviously often troubled going to God's presence.

First, remember that the ideal presented in Scripture really is the best. The degree that I have fallen short of it, obviously, corresponds to the damage I'm living with. Still, the ideal is beautiful, perfect, and the best for everyone. In facing the ideal given in God's Word I must remember that my failing to live up to it doesn't render it untrue. It renders me unfaithful. That realization followed by repentance helps me.

Second, and only after I faced the perfection of God's precepts, I can still take them wherever I am today. I can stand for what God has revealed and never fudge to excuse myself. I can love, support, and extend grace to my children as best I can and in all the opportunities the Lord gives me. Painful consequences may remain as God's principle of sowing and reaping is always intact. I can, though, seek His grace as His redemption can show up in the most amazing places. When the mess gets unruly and I become exasperated and crushed, when I've done everything I'm supposed to do, and when I don't know what else to do, I can lay it down at Jesus' feet. I can unload like these Pilgrims going to Jerusalem so I don't fail to get to the Jerusalem of God's presence where I must never forget I'm going.

Finally, I must keep my head on straight about my career and my financial situation. You are not your career; your career is just part of who you are as one who must work. You are not your financial status; your financial status is just a colorful detail of your story that in no way defines it. Some great life stories have had lots of money and others incredibly little while some pathetic life stories have been written in every possible financial status. Financial status, then, could never be the determining factor of how your life turns out so don't live as if it was. When the way gets rocky and money tight, seek the Lord first. You aren't a kingdom builder yourself, just a traveling pilgrim who won't even need one of life's dollars when you get where you're ultimately going. You don't really, then, want to "*labor in vain*", do you?

10

Blessed Is Everyone That Feareth The Lord

Psalm 128

"What's wrong with my home?", someone says. "I don't know about my marriage; My spouse and I just don't get along", says another. One has suffered though divorce, another has issues of a blended family, or another is adjusting to the death of a family member and everything has changed. "Children trample on your toes, but later trample on your heart", says some parent eaten up with disgust and heartbrokenness for how things have turned out. The point is not to scold those who have had family problems, but to realize that as pilgrims many of us are worried sick about these things. These things the pilgrim thought of as he traveled to Jerusalem, and so do many of us as we journey to the Lord's presence. In dealing with these concerns, we unearth a truth here that is really the secret of a successful Christian home: *"Blessed is everyone that feareth the Lord"*.

I. The Firm Foundation of a Christian Family (v. 1-2)

A. The Fear of God Is Necessary for Real Happiness

How well Psalm 128 follows Psalm 127, and is, in fact, its sequel. In Psalm 127 things were given valuation, but here we have a deeper reflection on the family and the key to it. One heavy burden on any pilgrim's heart is this burden of how his family will turn out or at least how the family will proceed from where we are today.. It's a burden that never changes from generation to generation.

The Psalm begins with the word *"blessed"*, which many people define as happy. The word is best described as contentment, or a real, deep, abiding happiness. We must stop and clarify our meaning here as the word "happiness" is defined in so many conflicting ways in our day. Clearly, we speak of more than an emotional burst of laughing. What we're talking about is something that settles much deeper and stays longer down in the heart.

"Blessed is everyone that feareth the Lord" tells us right away that the fear of the Lord is the foundation of the home and its happiness. We don't usually associate happiness with fear, but if it's the fear of the Lord we speak of, we should. If we would only truly fear the Lord, we would finally see that there is nothing else in life to fear at all. Since we're burdened about our families, pilgrim, I'm happy to report that this Psalm will show us some beautiful pictures of a Christian home, but we must begin at the beginning to have that kind of home – that beginning is the fear of the Lord. **As we saw in Psalm 127, we are presented with the ideal that is at once what our home life should be and what it will be judged by. Still, no matter where we are today, these descriptions presented are where we should turn at every possible opportunity. Where the brokenness won't allow us to go, we must turn to the Lord.**

Verse 1 goes on to say *"that walketh in his ways"*. That's an explanation of what the fear of the Lord is in relation to the home. The fear of the Lord isn't hiding when the thunder roars for fear of His lightning striking you, but rather believing what He says about sin, its effects, chastening, and believing it enough to obey. It's more accurate for us to see fear of the Lord as a deep reverence of God. At the end of the day, that will look something like obedience if our fear of the Lord is the real deal.

For the record, that reverence is the difference in a Christian family. Some ask, "why live right?" To answer that question, lift the roof off your home and look in. Do you see Christian love and joy, or a joyless place that lacks real contentment? As you can imagine, the stakes are high.

[Forgive the personal word, but I myself have experienced failings in my home. As I said before, some was caused by me and some by others. I deeply regret my part and know of brokenness. I

also know of the turbulence of mind, heart, and soul these Pilgrim Psalms address. I believed what these psalms taught before my own problems, but I believe them still. I don't rewrite the standard when I fall short of it, but I admit that I am wrong and how much better my life would be right now had I more closely heeded what is taught in this beautiful psalm. I am going to always firmly stand for what this psalm teaches even if my life could serve to some degree as a cautionary tale to reinforce it. Finally, I am going to boldly grasp how I can lay these heavy things down to go on to God's presence. I encourage all who has any sort of family brokenness to go along with me. I don't want my writings to be hypocritical, but I want to clearly bring out the text. I pray you will take it in that spirit.]

B. The Fear of God Is Necessary for Productive Labor

In verse 2 see the change from "*every one*" to "*thou*". Our subject gets more specific and personal. To be clear, Jesus is the answer for every home. Not a superficial acknowledgment of Christ, but a dynamic presence that says He is in charge. Psalm 127 told us of "*labor in vain*", but here the pilgrim can eat of his labor and financial gains. Blessing comes to those who fear (reverence) the Lord and do the work He has given them. We are not to be the rebel or sluggard but make our work fulfilling what He has told us to do.

"*Labor in vain*" is not the case for the God-fearing man who labors in God's calling, including the call the Lord gave him toward his family. It's only in the Lord that a pilgrim can ever enjoy the fruits of his labor. Things only ever have value in the context of God's will. The person who doesn't fear the Lord hasn't the ability to enjoy the good things of this life. No wonder many pilgrims are so troubled.

When it says "*happy shalt thou be*", before you write off that indescribable happiness, just remember that some Christians have found it true. Our struggles do not negate the principle; they only prove that we've not truly grasped the principle yet. This Psalm is not given as condemnation, but a call for the pilgrim to lay this needless burden down and step into the real joy of a Christian family that's found in the context of fearing the Lord. Notice the word *"well"*, which is the same as the word *"good"* in verse 1. That speaks of a security and peace your *"labor in vain"* could never achieve, and one that only the fear of the Lord can provide.

II. The Precious Blessing of a Christian Family (v. 3-4)

A. The Fear of God Provides Paradise on Earth

Here's a quote from long ago: "Adam had a home in Paradise and now man only has Paradise in the home." Sadly, many hate their homes and daydream of an exotic island in the sea as paradise. In reality, our paradise in this sinful world can only be found in the Christian home. Still, remember it's all tied to the fear of the Lord, not Christian appearances. A family that's a Christian home believes God together, attends church together, and seeks Him together. That's the point here.

It's true that one could sin and hurt the others trying to live in the fear of the Lord in a home, and what a shame that is; however, there's still value in fearing the Lord. Fearing the Lord by even one person in a home adds distinct value to it. If we strive for the ideal case where we all fear the Lord together, this Psalm shows us what our family could look like.

In a Christian home as God designed it, structure is rigid while the blessings are expansive. First, the wife is a great blessing in such a home. The inverse of this fact is true for a God-fearing wife in her having the blessing of the husband, but as always is the case in the Bible, the husband is reminded of what a great blessing his wife is.

When it mentions *"fruitful vine"*, the text is describing the scene that was common in those days. Vines grew near homes to provide both beauty and fruit. That is God's plan for the wife in a Christian home. As you can guess, fruit refers to bearing godly children.[8] There's no doubt that we're in a section of Scripture here that drives the world crazy. Pilgrim, before we decide to agree with the world on this matter, we should examine their homes and decide

---

[8] Of course, there are compensations to childless homes in Christ.

if that's what we really want. I'm guessing that's not what you want when you compare what's described here – contentment and deep happiness. Some of us know by experience it's not best.

More than children are in view here. As Song of Solomon 7:8 says, "*I said, I will go up to the palm tree, I will take hold of the boughs thereof: now also thy breasts shall be as clusters of the vine, and the smell of thy nose like apples.*" Love and physical pleasure in intimacy without guilt, and within God's boundaries, serves as a source of this deep happiness and contentment. The God-fearing man can find more happiness in one woman than a man who doesn't fear the Lord can find in dozens! Watch out for Satan's darts, his appeals to our old flesh, and the temptation he sends our way. The Marilyn Monroe's of the world (or those like her) may catch our eye, or incite our lust, but can never reach the heart on the level that God designed the wife to be in the Christian home. To take that type of woman, the trashy woman, could at best only trash up our lives until real happiness cannot be found Though it grates the world, let's remember she's a tender vine, and not an oak tree; so, treat her accordingly. Of course, all of this is a fairytale if you don't fear the Lord.

Another thing about a vine is that it clings to the home. In this case, the vine would hold fast to the sides of the house just as in a real Christian home, the wife clings to her home, her husband, and her children. She's not like the strange woman of Proverbs 7:11 described as "*loud and stubborn; her feet abide not in her house*". This is not necessarily teaching that a woman could never work outside the home, but that the Lord must be sought by every husband and wife for His will. If you think about it, even the oft debated phrase in Titus 2:5 of "*keeper at home*" suggests attachment to it. Husbands should treat wives with real love as if they are a treasure. If you are still doubting that they are a treasure, just remember that God consistently said they were in our lives. We find ourselves in so many different circumstances in the pain-filled world, but we should see this as the way it ought to be and honor it as much as possible.

Psalm 127 said children were a blessing and they're brought into this as well. *"Olive plants round about thy table"* speaks of children. Olive trees are tough, send up sprouts to replace itself, and are an oil of gladness. This analogy reminds you of the full quiver in Psalm 127, but here children specifically are said to give joy. Some children are not a joy, but *"train up a child"* is God's plan for that situation. Again, this is not a guarantee for perfect children, but God's methods always produce better results than do others. Let's not stop, then, until we enjoy our children, stepchildren, grandchildren, etc. Whatever it takes, we are not where we need to be until our children have become a true source of joy in our lives. Pilgrim, look at that table, the giggling voices, the wife, and see the glimpse of happiness the Lord designed men to crave. The wives and the children deserve it, and the fear of the Lord demands it.

B. The Fear of God Must Be Emphasized

Verse 4 repeats verse 2 so that we would not miss the emphasis of how the burdens we carry about our homes are lifted. These great blessings are the promise to those truly having the fear of the Lord in their home. Verse 4 opens with *"behold"* almost as if we are to be in awe of what was just said in verses 2 and 3. In this fear of the Lord and its corresponding obedience, the Lord gives far more in blessings than the cost of that reverence and obedience. Everyone wants a gimmick, and even Christians search the Bible for quick fixes for marriage or children's issues. Though there is help in the Bible for both of those issues, you can't skip the foundational fear of the Lord.

I read where W. Graham Scroggie, another preacher of yesteryear, told the story of the famous song "Home Sweet Home" that was written by John Howard Payne. The strange case about that sentimental song is that Mr. Payne was a fake. He never had a good home in his life. Once when he was homeless, he heard a family singing and wrote the song about something he never actually had. Later, he died a lonely man in Africa. Pilgrim, we need the real thing, not merely the sentiment.

II. The Abiding Joys of a Christian Family (v. 5-6)

A. The Fear of God Gives Ongoing Blessings

When we read "*the Lord shall bless thee out of Zion*", we are reminded that Zion is God's headquarters to these Jewish pilgrims. They'd sense that peace as they topped the hills and saw the city of Jerusalem in the distance. Pilgrim, we look to Heaven, or our private time with the Lord here, and that's where our blessings come from.

The text also says that we will "*see the good of Jerusalem all the days of thy life*". I want to see good to my end, whatever the days of my life may be, don't you? This way, and only this way, can we see that good. So, pilgrim, let's fear the Lord and obey Him even in our homes no matter where we're starting from today. Look how little the city of Jerusalem feared the Lord in Jesus' day, and she was destroyed just a few decades later. This issue is so serious that it's ridiculous that we think our homes can succeed without the fear of the Lord.

B. The Fear of God Gives Lasting Blessings

In life, we often talk of something's staying power. In fact, we often gauge something's value by how long it can last. The Old Testament spoke of prosperity and long life while the New Testament talks of adversity and a life for Christ. You may doubt the veracity of this promise when you think of some godly people who didn't live long enough to see their grandchildren. Remember, it's the quality of life, not the quantity, that matters. It's what you see in your grandchildren, not how long you see them. O how we ought to desire to see the third generation of our Christian homes serving Christ, especially as we live in a day when most of these third generations are near heathen.

We can't escape the fact that for each generation it's always tied the fear of the Lord, obedience, and sincerity. Considering that fact, it's time that we be real about it. With the fear of the Lord, we can see our children's children, even if it's from heaven. You can see them follow the Lord, which is <u>all</u> that matters. You can see the fear of the Lord mold a family and do something that even death can't hurt! We have be faithful today, no matter the past. We can love and encourage our children no matter what brokenness exists. All steps of following these principles will yield eternal results.

As we said before, one spouse or parent can fail in the matter of the fear of the Lord and hurt everyone under that roof, but your fearing the Lord will be a positive help. Again, the fear of the Lord in even one person can only make things better. The last part of the promise says," *and peace upon Israel*". It turns out that if we fear the Lord, and have a Christian family, that we will even bless our nation.

If you look at what's out there, you'll see there's a lot of messes. Some homes are a war zone, and others are some better but lack any real happiness or contentment. Such a home will burden the pilgrims traveling to the presence of the Lord in detrimental ways. Pilgrim, it doesn't have to be that way for us. We can turn toward the Lord today no matter our situation. The best single piece of information on a happy Christian family that we have is this simple thought: *"Blessed is every one that feareth the Lord"*.

11

Many a Time Have They Afflicted Me

Psalm 129

Here's another of the Pilgrim Psalms ("*Song of degrees*") that the pilgrims sing as they travel to Jerusalem and to the very Have you ever gotten off by yourself and given deep thought to the trouble, trial, and affliction you have experienced in your life? If you have, what conclusions did you come up with? About yourself? About the enemies who hurt you? About the Lord Himself? Instead of leading us to negative thoughts, such a review of the pain suffered at the hands of our bitterest enemies should ultimately lead us to thoughts of our Lord. There are some things the weary pilgrim needs before this inevitable history is given: "*Many a time have they afflicted me.*"

I. The Afflictions of God's People (v. 1-3)

A. The Constancy of Trouble

presence of God. Don't be surprised if you notice in this Psalm similarities to Psalm 124 as the issue of dealing with bitter enemies is of such powerful emotion that another song is needed for the pilgrims, only this time with a twist. Here the afflicting enemies hit us with persecution. In fact, afflictions at the hands of others will likely consume your thoughts more than any other problem, perhaps, because the sinful response of hate ever stands ready to throw gasoline on its fire.

As the pilgrim walks and meditates on his personal troubles, his thoughts shift to the troubles of his people, here the nation of Israel, and all that she has suffered. Clearly, Israel, the Lord's earthly people, are the true interpretation of this Psalm. Still, this Psalm is for all the saved, who are pilgrims heading to a heavenly city.

Just like Psalm124, this Psalm also provides no clue to establish its timeframe. The situation for when it was written is unrevealed so that we may apply its truths to any time or situation we may face. Despite the inability to locate a specific event, we know that Israel has had a long history of this type of affliction. Because of the intensity of the affliction being tied at times to the fact of her relationship to the Lord, it can accurately be called persecution. *"Many a time have they afflicted me"*– though at times her suffering has been over mistakes she has made, many episodes of affliction were from enemies who simply hated her God and persecuted her.

While no pinpointed time is given, an origination is here where it says, *"from my youth"*. That goes all the way back to Egypt. Couple *"from my youth"* with *"many a time"* and you see her affliction began early and has always been around. In fact, it continues to our day.

I love that the *"they"* are never specified, though we can line up a long line of suspects. We don't know who *"they"* are. Apparently *"they"* are so inconsequential and meaningless that when a longer look is taken, *"they"* aren't even worth mentioning. Whoever *"they"* are, *"they"* afflicted this pilgrim.

As God's people, we too have all faced affliction from others, and some of that affliction has even been persecution from His enemies. Most of us can say *"from my youth"* as well since in many of our situations that affliction started when we were young in the faith. For example, family or friends have fought our faith, etc. We can fall in with *"many a time"* too as these afflictions have happened often and continue to the present day as well.

Verse 2 repeats *"many a time have they afflicted me"* to emphasize that affliction and persecution come often. When verse 1 ends with *"now may Israel say"*, it appears the soloist calls on the choir to join the song.[9] We are uplifted when verse 2 adds, *"yet they have not prevailed against me"*. Yes, *"they"* afflicted me, but *"they"* did not prevail – praise His Name! That little word *"yet"* is one we all need to write in stone and never forget. No doubt at times it looked like *"they"* would prevail, but *"they"* did not. This recalls the triumphant Matthew 16:18: *"And I say also unto thee, That thou art Peter, and upon this rock I will build my church; and the gates of hell shall not prevail against it."*

B. The Crack of the Whip

The pain of relentless affliction flying at you is learned in youth for sure, but in verse 3 it gets more specific – some of this affliction is deeply painful. The metaphor used here is of the whip. The whip would dig in like a plow plowing up ridges on your back. The word *"long"* highlights that the furrows on the back were made longer and even cross the whole back. The point of that description is that this affliction prolongs the pain by taking longer and is something akin to torture.

God's enemies may not have prevailed against us, but it wasn't for lack of trying! For that matter, the pain was quite severe too. Israel has always faced this painful persecution, through the New Testament and into modern history. One of the most heinous examples would be Hitler and Nazi Germany attempting to eradicate the Jews, and actually killing 6 million of them.

---

[9] You may recall this exact phrase from Psalm 124.

For that matter, we should consider Christ Who was whipped as a prelude to His crucifixion, though Jesus ultimately did His suffering for us. By Acts 5, the Apostles too faced the whip. By Acts 7, Stephen is stoned and from there we have seen a steady stream of beatings and martyrdom all the way to our present day. The atrocities we have seen perpetrated by ISIS against Christians in our day is a case in point. Again, this affliction is specifically persecution. We may not have all faced a literal whip, but, perhaps, you and I have felt the sting of God's enemies in our lives.

II. The Character of God Himself (v.4)

A. He Operates in Righteousness

There's one key fact here that stands above all this persecution – *"The Lord is righteous"*. Our very hearts cry out that it simply wouldn't be right if these enemies ultimately prevailed. Fortunately, verse 2 already told us that they did not. If they did ultimately prevail, we wouldn't be able to believe that our Holy God really holds the universe in the palm of His hand. You see, our God is righteous and that finally demands the doom of His enemies. His righteousness demands He act.

B. He Times Our Trials

Though the Lord's righteousness demands He act, the timing of His action is His domain. Many err in thinking that the Lord isn't righteous because evil appears to prevail, but hold on, it doesn't prevail. Evil prevails for a time, yes; forever, no. *"He hath cut asunder the chords of the wicked."* You see, He hath cut the cord of that evil. It didn't hold forever! Some hold that this cord refers to the one that holds the ox to the plow, but that analogy is clearly not carried beyond verse 3. No, this *"cord"* refers to the one that holds us so *"they"* can afflict us.

This cord that binds us could be any number of things – a strong army, the control of key goods needed for survival, a position of authority, etc. – but whatever it is, this cord makes it possible for them to afflict us. When the Lord cuts this cord, He is cutting their ability to afflict us. What we often fail to see is that He reaches down and cuts when He <u>knows</u> we've had enough. Though the Lord often gets a bad rap, and though we are horribly forgetful, this fact is indisputable. We should pause here and praise His Name.

In our personal lives *"many a time"* we think we are sunk, but we're still here. Egypt didn't hold Israel forever. For that matter, neither did Hitler and Nazi Germany, nor any other. Why? The Lord cut the cord! Here is an accurate look back at history and a trustworthy way to look at the future. When it is time, our Lord will cut the cord!

By the Lord's perfect timing, His people are strengthened by affliction and persecution. Of course, this is the piece of the puzzle that we are constantly misplacing. This fact has been proven repeatedly as God's people have survived when others have vanished. Israel exists though she has faced the worst of affliction and persecution, but what of Edom, Assyria, or Nazi Germany? The wicked swing their hammer, but God's Word becomes the anvil that shatters it!

III. The Withering of God's Enemies (v. 5-8)

A. The Prayer for God's Will

Verses 5-8 developed the thought for our encouragement of just how thoroughly the Lord has cut the cords of those who *"many a time"* want to persecute us. This encouragement begins as a prayer against these enemies. This psalm is a minor example of what we find more prevalent in several other of the Psalms. These type Psalms are known as the Imprecatory Psalms. These Psalms are those where the Psalmist asked the Lord to do something negative to his enemies, enemies who ultimately were the enemies of the Lord. If you do much reading, you will notice that this type of Psalms set the critics off! A more careful look at this Psalm and those like it will help us realize that they need not shock our sensibilities at all.

The Pilgrim in this Psalm, just like those in other of the Imprecatory Psalms, is praying that the enemies of the Lord be confounded and turned back and not be successful in what they clearly would like to do. This prayer is asking for the Lord, Who is righteous (verse 4), to be God and do what God does. What is it that He always does? He always ultimately turns His enemies around from their chosen path and desired results. He does not allow their plans to succeed. Since the Lord will respond this way no matter what anyway, this prayer is but an encouragement and an agreement with the Lord because He is righteous, and we know what He will do when His time is right. Again, nothing is really asked for in this prayer that is not going to happen anyway.

That little phrase at the end of verse 5 ("*that hate Zion*") is the clue that explains the righteousness of this prayer to a holy God. There's a clear message here to all people. That simple message is that there's a consequence for hating the Lord and His people! There's an obvious reason too why this prayer is not a wicked one. Can't you see what it is? It's not wicked because its alternative would be for wickedness to prevail and God to fail! In that light, it's one of the most logical and righteous prayers imaginable.

B. The Completeness of Their Failure

At first glance, verses 6 and 7 might seem obscure. In Bible times dirt was often used on the flat roof of houses. A seed could land on that dirt roof and sprout up but would always wither before it grew up to be worth anything. In some cases, it could be a seed of something worthwhile to have like wheat, but the sprout could never make it to harvest. This metaphor is a picture of how powerless God's enemies who "*many a time have they afflicted me*" really are. The sun of God's holiness always withers them. "*They*" are quick to sprout up, look capable of much, but they quickly wither. It is always so with God's enemies. Even in our day when world leaders make their grandiose statements, it's simply the stage after they have sprung up, but before they're scorched.

Verse 7 continues the metaphor. As great as we assumed the sprouts would be, they provide no harvest. They fell short of expectations. They had no staying power despite our fears. Just look at that withered, worthless grass now. When the text says, "… *nor he that bindeth sheaves his bosom*", it refers to a person's lap or the fold of the robe pulled up to carry. How well I remember my

Grandmother pulling up her apron to carry things in its fold. I even tried carrying our eggs that way in my pulled-up shirt, and it worked beautifully until I tripped returning from the barn. Not only was there nothing for the hand to grab, but there's also nothing to carry back in the fold of the robe. It was a lively sprout, but now it's nothing. The point is simple: no harvest from a plan against God's people can ever come in! By harvest time, the seed's sprout is gone.

In verse 8, we see a form of the word "*bless*" used two times. That word recalls the custom of what was often said at harvest time. Something so ancient that even Boaz said it to his men in Ruth 2:4. We're being told here that the blessing so common to all pilgrims in Old Testament times will not be said by this pilgrim to these persecutors. How could he? We would never bless those fighting the Lord and his people, would we? That would be a shameful sin. In addition, as we have already seen, by harvest time there's nothing left to bless! You see, the Lord hasn't blessed them and now it's too late. In other words, He is righteous and has already destroyed them.

Can't you see that having thought this through, as in this Song of Degrees, that this pilgrim will find it much easier to go on to Jerusalem? Doesn't it make the journey to God's presence much easier for we modern-day pilgrims as well? We can lay this burden down and travel on because while their harvest will not come in, ours most definitely will come in through Jesus Christ. This Psalm can help us the next time we survey our lives on the way to God's presence and opine: "*many a time have they afflicted me.*"

12

Out of the Depths

Psalm 130

Have you ever been at the bottom? Have you ever been so far down that you couldn't even see the way back up? Were your own mistakes and failures behind that downward spiral? That's exactly where the Pilgrim Psalmist was in this Psalm, and as all the pilgrims in these Songs of Ascent, he had issues as he traveled to the presence of God in Jerusalem. We can learn from him in the way he came up from the dark place, but first we can be instructed also on how he began at the very bottom as he speaks to us *"out of the depths."*

I. Seeking the Lord from the Depths (v. 1-3)

A. He Prayed

The Pilgrim sings in this 11th Pilgrim Psalm and it's no wonder he is hindered from the presence of the Lord. You might say his song begins as a tearjerker as we visualize him with red eyes, runny nose, and his being all torn up. Perhaps he goes the lowest of any pilgrim in these Psalms. As we will soon see, it appears this traveling pilgrim will have to face deep soul crisis to again worship in the presence of the Lord.

There is so much to glean here. Don't ever believe, if you ever find yourself looking from *"out of the depths"*, that you have reached a place to throw in the towel. If we travel with this pilgrim all the way through this Pilgrim Psalm, we will see that the depths are simply a more intense, compelling place to seek His presence.

Notice that in the entirety of this Psalm an individual speaks. That makes sense as it is an incredibly personal, individual matter. You will also notice a lot of "*I*" and "*my*" all the way through verse 6. The choir sits on the sidelines and listens to the soloist in this one. We also notice, as we have in several other of these Pilgrim Psalms, that we know nothing of the time or place of this Psalm. All we know for sure is that the pilgrim sits on the edge, if you will, and is falling into despair.

"*Depths*" carries a more ominous meaning than we might imagine. It speaks of something that is deep and unsearchable. In Scripture, it's always used in conjunction with a great body of water like the ocean, and therefore suggests complete chaos and helplessness. The Israelites were never a seagoing people and they could be classified as a people generally spooked by the deep. In addition, this was the days before Marine science could estimate the depths of the sea in any way. For these Israelites, nothing seemed so deep, or so inducing of helplessness, as the sea. As it's used here, it's the perfect description of a soul in its deepest trouble.[10] In fact, this pilgrim wouldn't be the only Israelite who ever swirled in the depths. The famous prophet Jonah had the ultimate terrors in the depths.[11]

While much of what this pilgrim says in this Psalm would seem the perfect thing to say to an unsaved person who didn't know the Lord, we must not forget that he's a pilgrim, a believer in the Lord. Don't let anyone kid you: a Christian can go to the depths! To visualize it, think of the lowest place our soul can go, a place where we feel removed from the Lord. It's a truth the Lord made sure we do not miss in His Word as so many people on its pages went to the depths.

There's a variety of situations that could take us to the depths – a heavy loss, horrific affliction, a time of depression, or a crushed heart. Still, there's one more major category that could take us to the depths. Can you think of what we've missed? It's that place where

---

[10] Compare Psalms 42:7 and 88:7.

[11] See Jonah 2 to read of that harrowing experience.

we blown it, where we've messed up everything, where we've sinned. Maybe you know from personal experience that personal failure is some of the heaviest affliction that we could ever go through. To make this an even more critical issue, we should see that more of our affliction comes from our own error than we've ever allowed ourselves to think. In fact, it can turn into a virtual field of land mines on the way to the presence of the Lord.

From *"out of the depths"* he said, *"have I cried unto thee, O Lord."* That was true on every level. No doubt he wept. No doubt he cried out from a heavy heart since he's way down in the depths. These depths have peculiar, unexpected traits. Nothing about the depths matches our predictions. In fact, we easily get in, but find it's not quite so easy to get out. We imagine we won't get in, and prophesy if we do we'll just jump out, but then we find out about the Herculean grip of the depths. In truth, we often run headlong into the depths. Now that we're here, our pleasures have vanished, our plans have failed, and our manipulations have blown up in our faces. We ran the gauntlet of self-will and the blades of consequence have taken us down.

Despite our obvious, ugly analysis, there's something wonderful here. From *"out of the depths"* this pilgrim has cried out to the Lord – good move! This is one of the seven great Penitential Psalms.[12] The depths are so bad that he can't pull himself out, but he can cry out to the Lord. How low are you? How deep in the depths? Look up to the Lord. There's never a depth so deep the Lord can't hear you!

With our track record of spiritual dullness and prayerlessness, it may take the depths to get us to real prayer. We may struggle to pray in normal times, but we'll pray when we're sinking. That's exactly what this pilgrim is doing in verse 2. He begs the Lord to listen. Do you notice even his double emphasis as his emotions are all in on this prayer? It's as if he begs and then asks the Lord to bend His ear even closer. Don't be critical or harsh here – pilgrims have the privilege to pray. In another place, a different

[12] The others being Psalm 6, 32, 38, 51, 102, and 142.

Psalmist expressed what he found true of the Lord to whom this pilgrim prays; that other Psalmist once said *"... If I make my bed in hell, behold, thou art there"* (Psalm 139:8).

B. He Thinks of His Sin

He begins verse 3, *"If thou, Lord."* In these depths, he begins to think seriously and deeply about the Lord and then about himself. Obviously, he had not been thinking deeply about either himself or the Lord before or he wouldn't have landed in the depths. Now, in a wise move for any pilgrim, he reflects on the character of God. If you have read these Pilgrim Psalms in order, you've already seen how the pilgrim in his different situations comes to reflect on the character of God. We can take that as a life principle – digging into the character of God is part of the solution to all my problems.

In further proof of how intensely he's thinking about the Lord, notice the variety of God's names he uses as he cries out to Him. He alternates between the names as well. He uses LORD (Jehovah) 4 times because He's the great and mighty I AM, Covenant God of Israel. He uses Lord (Adonai) 3 times because He is the Lord and Master of all. He also uses LORD (Jah) once here only in verse 3 because of His majesty and His almost frightening holy nature. He's clearly on the right track in what he's thinking about his Lord.

He then begins thinking of his standing with the Lord, of who he really is, and the path of his own sin that sent him down into the depths. He asks rhetorically. *"If thou, LORD, shouldst mark iniquities...?"* *"Shouldst mark"* means "take account or keep count." He makes a double observation here. He sees himself corrupted with sin and without excuse, even in the current mess. In addition, he realizes that if the Lord looked on us in His holiness, counted our sins, and did nothing on our behalf, we couldn't stand – we'd be destroyed. Yes, if He takes account, we're doomed.

How ridiculous we usually are about this matter of sin. We often belittle sin, laugh it off, underestimate it, but that's not a luxury we can have when we're in the depths. In the depths, it all gets clearer. How bad is it? Think of Calvary! My sins were so grotesque that the impeccable Jesus Christ had to suffer and die for my sins. Being a pilgrim, that was a past tense matter for him. We believers too realize that we have already received Christ as Savior. What is lost when we lack spiritual lucidity is that my sins and my Savior are present-tense truths as well.

Of course, we can't stand if the Lord calls out our sins. It's not really a hypothetical thought to this pilgrim either. Consequences are catching up to him and crushing him like he already can't stand because of his sins. Have you ever been there, Christian pilgrim? It's almost as if the depths are even lower now. I've been there. I've been in the low place, thought about God and myself, and then saw myself standing in the putrid filth of my sins. Still, and what we are soon to see in this Pilgrim Psalm, it's at this point of greatest depth that we are ready for help.

II. Seeing the Lord in the Depths (v. 4-6)

A. He Thinks of Forgiveness

Such a realistic, crushing look at sin is good for us because of where it automatically pushes us to look next. Verse 4 has the colossal hinge: "*But*". That hinge transports us. I've seen Him in His holiness, which exposed me, and now I can look to His mercy. "*But there is forgiveness with thee*" is a string of beautiful words. That's a phrase that we could be theologically correct in sharing with an unsaved person. It's also a phrase that could describe what happened the day I was born again. Don't miss, however, one of the most beautiful words in that phrase. It is the little word "*is*." Praise His name, this phrase is as true for me today as it was back there on that day I received Jesus Christ as my Savior. Romans 5:1 ("*Therefore being justified by faith, we have peace with God through our Lord Jesus Christ:*") is as accurate today as it was the day I passed from death into life. The great theme of Scripture – my sin and His forgiveness – that touched me when I was saved can bless me again when I've blown it.

We see, too, the parameters of the beautiful word *"forgiveness."* It is bound on every side by *"with thee."* We must never forget that. We must see that it's not in us, pilgrim, or we'll forever linger in the depths. That truth of His being the single source of forgiveness is so exact that I don't even need to say that I should forgive myself. I've said that before but misunderstood the point. Sometimes I need to not be satisfied in the depths and that requires dealing with me, but it's not a matter of me forgiving myself. I'm not God! Forgiveness is only with Him! I don't need my forgiveness; I need His!

That statement of forgiveness is followed by: *"that thou mayest be feared."* We see here the natural progression from forgiveness to fear, a fear that means reverential awe, is a good, but respectable thing for us to have. Can't you see what this means? The fear of the Lord, or sincere respect of Him, was certainly out the window in whatever matter landed me in the depths, but now that respect is back. The Lord knows this pilgrim is in the depths, He knows why this pilgrim is in the depths, and He forgave him! Praise His name!

B. He Waited on the Lord

The Lord forgives. This mercy turns the thoughts of the erring pilgrim in the depths as he realizes that he can wait on the Lord because of Who He is. The multiple uses of the word *"wait"* suggests the road the forgiven pilgrim must travel. He says, *"my soul doth wait"*, and so there's nothing superficial now. When the pilgrim references *"his word"* he's saying, I don't deserve the Lord's promises, but since I can depend on them, I will wait on Him for their fulfillment. Let's follow the pilgrim's lead and wait on the Lord because there's no one else to wait on! Wait on the Lord because His character says that He will come. The Lord is the way out of the depths. We travel a rugged journey to this obvious truth.

In verse 6 we listen to this pilgrim in the depths as he's now waiting on the Lord like a man waits for a new day. He watches like someone on the night watch might be looking. In our day, he'd be like the person on night shift sneaking glances out the window for first light; or he's like someone suffering in sickness thinking, if I can just wait till morning. What is it about the morning? It always comes! It comes fresh and new! Just like the Lord! As Lamentations 3:22-23 says, *"It is of the LORD'S mercies that we are not consumed, because his compassions fail not. They are new every morning: great is thy faithfulness."*

Waiting isn't working, it's trusting; it isn't taking matters into your own hands, it's leaving them in the Lord's hands. The repetition in verse 6 shows the intensity of his growing faith to wait on the Lord.

III. Speaking of the Lord from the Depths (v. 7-8)

A. He Thinks of Others

The pilgrim is still in the depths. Do you read anything here of the depths going away? No, he's waiting, and the Lord hasn't yet removed his afflictions or consequences. His body still speaks *"out of the depths"*, but his soul apparently isn't quite so low. He now thinks of others. He now speaks of Israel, which is community for him. When we have really met with the Lord, even in the depths, we will begin to think of others. We aren't, as you can surely see, the only person in the depths. Look around, pilgrim, there are other believers in that dreadful place. Sin has done a number on us all.

The Pilgrim sees beyond himself to his people. He knows the Lord has given him mercy and has enough mercy for Israel too. I pray you and I won't miss that eternal truth in our days. You see, it's the mercy and grace of God that conquers the depths! After we're as assured as he is, let's tell others as well. Israel, or all of God's people, has the strongest hope.

B. He Thinks of Redemption

There are two reasons for hope mentioned here: a) mercy, and b) plenteous redemption. Wow, the Lord is merciful and has the plenteous redemption to back it up! *"Plenteous redemption"* is an extraordinarily beautiful expression that highlights that there is more than enough for everyone – little ole me in the depths and everyone else.

As it turns out, Israel, an example he cares about, is the perfect illustration. Israel has often been in the depths and the Lord has repeatedly brought her up out of the deepest depths. Whether it was when she was in the bondage of Egypt, or the vicious cycle of the time of the Judges, or the horrific Babylonian Captivity, Israel has lived out the truth of this Psalm.

Perhaps it's already crossed your mind that there's an application for the unsaved here that we can rejoice over. There's plenteous redemption for the soul headed to the depths of hell! Hallelujah! Still, we must not forget that this Psalm is written for the pilgrim. The Lord will do for your Christian life in the depths brought on by your own failure exactly what He did when your soul was in the vortex that pulled you toward Hell.

Can you see it now? The depths are not the end of the story. That's what we thought and that's why the depths are so horrifying. No, the depths are not the end of the story – redemption is! Our Lord will finally, completely, deliver His people! Take that to heart, pilgrim, as you may need it someday, if not already.

This pilgrim can go to Jerusalem to worship because he is already worshiping. The presence of God, here he comes! Let's you and I allow Psalm 130 to be the blueprint for the next time we mess up and must call on the Lord *"out of the depths!"*

13

Things Too High for Me

Psalm 131

Where do you and I stand regarding pride and ambition? Since pride and ambition are the common lot of sinful flesh, the question is not, do you have it, but what progress have you made against it? We must do the hard thing for us, as David did, the thing all weary pilgrims so need to do. We need to come face-to-face with *"things too high for me"*.

I. What the Lord Helped Take from Me (v. 1)

A. Pride

The traveling pilgrim has another issue hindering him from joyously going to the presence of the Lord. This 12th Pilgrim Psalm is unique as it is the first one to deal with something that we pilgrims often don't even realize at first. In fact, it may have popped up as something discovered when the other issues of these Psalms were faced. Since we are fresh off Psalm 130, maybe when we came up *"out of the depths"*, we were humbled and found out the subject of this Psalm.

This psalm is specifically labeled *"a song of degrees of David"*. Along with Psalms 122 and 124, this Psalm is only the third one to specifically designate David. His life is to be used as the example here. Musically, this Psalm is another solo, the choir is idle, and perhaps we should get alone and sing it till its truths are faced in our lives.

David begins: *"Lord, my heart is not haughty."* *"Haughty"* simply means to be lifted up in pride. No time is wasted in this Psalm in revealing that its issue is pride. Notice all the words that suggest pride: *"haughty"*, *"lofty"*, *"great matters"*, and *"too high"*. Some think this was when either Michal or Saul accused him of pride, but if you review those stories in Scripture you see that he really wasn't all that prideful in those episodes. In fact, if the problem of which he writes was no more than that someone had accused him of pride, or just that he had gotten over pride, this Psalm would itself be prideful.

Verse 2 will later reveal that this was an experience learned the hard way. What we have here is David humbly confessing that he had been so prideful. This pride hindered him from going to God's presence. Even though this pride is not as obvious as the affliction discussed in other Pilgrim Psalms, it was just as real. My guess is that this episode refers to his later years when he numbered the people in an ugly episode of pride. Apparently, after years of humility, it finally got to them. A shepherd boy, now a great king with a terrific military record, had pride catch up with him even though he was an older man.

Some people have pride based on nothing while others, like David, develop pride over real accomplishment. Even if the accomplishment was overrated from the divine perspective, it was still accomplishment. Perhaps you, as I, have seen pride catch up to people late in life. I've read sermons from the younger days of a preacher and then find sermons from his older days and the difference is huge. Not only was the difference massive, but it was also disgusting. What David is saying here is that he had been prideful and now he reflects on that ugly episode that the Lord had graciously delivered him from after much damage.

When David said, *"my heart"*, he spoke of necessity. Change had to be in the heart since that's the place where pride began. Psalm 101:5b says, *"him that hath an high look and a proud heart I will not suffer*". No, it's something the Lord cannot allow, and that makes it's obviously a problem for any pilgrim!

David further said, *"nor mine eyes lofty"*. That makes sense also as it's the heart that looks through the eyes. That phrase reminds us of a saying in our day – the phrase "looking down our noses". That means exactly what you visualize as a person raises his or her head so high that they must look down their nose to see you. As you can imagine, pride uses sight because it has so little regard for faith.

Don't lose sight here that the negative is being reviewed to bring the positive to light. *"Not"* …" *nor*" …" *neither*" … Praise the Lord, David was helped. Humility was the tonic the Lord poured into his soul.

B. Ambition

The phrase *"neither do I exercise myself in great matters"* is incisive. The word *"exercise"* means involve and even carries the idea of meddling. *"Great matters"* speaks of something significant. Though not exclusively, it is a word often used of the Lord where it makes far more sense. In other words, it's something that catches our fancy and our ambition overrides obedience. We are in these *"great matters"* because we like them simply for their greatness, or significance, not because it's what the Lord wants.

We fear insignificance more than anything, yet we haven't the heavenly perspective to even know what's truly significant. In our confusion, we then sink to the low level of worldly significance. Carrying out the absurd process, we even superimpose it upon Christianity. What the world calls significant is anathema to Christianity, yet we mistakenly believe it is Christianity itself. Then we live for personal greatness; we become ambitious. The ambition that we suppose is for God's glory is merely our own craving of greatness, honor, or fame. At that point, what a treacherous detour we confuse for the highway of the Christian life.

We pilgrims need purpose rather than ambition. The right purpose is when we keep our heads on straight, with the end in view, and our focus on God's will. Though purpose has been a buzzword in our generation, we've lost our ability to distinguish it from ambition. For example, we might begin with a worthy purpose of reaching people for Christ but disintegrate into a craving for numbers to publicize. While purpose is praiseworthy, ambition can mess up a pilgrim!

Such ambition will eventually change us into an envious person who will be unable to root for anyone who does the same thing for the Lord that we do. For example, a preacher might not be able to enjoy a good sermon because he's afraid it's better than his sermon was. Or worse, we will be unable to pray for people with the same intensity we pray for ourselves because they have become competitors to us. In that process, we quit focusing on what honors the Lord and grow consumed with what elevates us. That may further degenerate to growing selfish or becoming a schemer to fulfill our ambitions. Finally, it becomes presumption, or as stated here: *"things too high for me"*.

"Things too high" has quite a ring, doesn't it? It's one word in the Hebrew language that means something extraordinary. It further carries the idea of something that's too great or difficult, or even something beyond me. It's funny how that works. On the one hand, I might have no problem accepting that I can't perform brain surgery. Brain surgery is beyond me, of course, and I have no trouble admitting it. On the other hand, I might think I'm amazingly spiritual, or discerning, or able to fix people. I'll think I'm the Bible expert, or the best teacher, or the greatest prayer warrior, and finally, I'll just believe the Lord likes me best! Can't you see it? *"Things too high for me"*!

There are some things beyond me and it's best I realize it. We finally need to learn that we can't do everything we think or want, even if popular psychology says otherwise. We're told constantly in our day that we can do anything we want to do. I'm not suggesting that we not try hard to challenge ourselves, but we cannot do everything we want to do. Some will never be a famous movie star or music sensation no matter how many times they tell themselves they will be. Others will never be the CEO of a great company. I remember someone I love once telling me that I could probably never be the pastor of one of those mega-churches with

10,000 people. As they put it, I didn't have the gifts or personality for that. To my shame, I remember it hurt my feelings, but do you want to know the truth? I realize now that I couldn't do it.

As we said before, this realization is no excuse to not do what the Lord has enabled you to do, but simply to realize that you exhaust your talents far more quickly than you imagine. There's even more to glean from *"things too high for me"*– some things are exclusively God's domain. No matter how seductive our ambitious thoughts may be, we cannot take the Lord's role in someone else's life. If that were not enough, there's also the little problem that there's many things we'll never understand here. Like David, or that publican in private prayer that Jesus told us about, let's chuck pride and ambition with the Lord's help.

II. What the Process Was Like (v. 2)

A. Quietness

The great need of we who jump into *"things too high for me"* is described here as being behaved and quieted. The word *"behaved"* means stilled, and carries the idea of finally lying down, or finally calming down after a time of charging ahead. *"Quieted"* meant originally to make level and carries the idea of calming down as well. Think about it. When we're too high, we need leveled off. What a mess, what a boisterous, frantic pace pride and ambition throw us into.

If you look back at the story of David numbering the people, you see a turbulent soul that quieted itself in surrender to God and returning to His will. David wasn't seeking *"things too high for me"* now because he had learned his place. He was a man who again said that he owed every good thing in himself to the Lord. Like him, many of us pilgrims are in desperate need of being leveled off.

B. Weaning

Next, we encounter the metaphor of *"as a child that is weaned of his mother"*. That comparison to a child is likely used because no matter your age, pride and ambition are childish. In this case, David is admitting that he was childish, so the metaphor of a child is perfect. The analogy used is that of a baby being weaned from his or her mother's breast. Many parents can visualize the scene of the hungry baby who acts as if he or she can't survive for another moment. As a dad, I remember all six of my children back in their nursing days falling apart before my wife, Alicia, could prepare herself to feed them. As she would stop what she's doing, or lie down, or adjust her clothing, they would grope and scream. The point here is that the prideful, ambitious pilgrim often carries on just as much!

I also vividly remember those days when my wife and I would decide that the baby must be weaned. My wife was especially astute at knowing when that point was reached. Perhaps you could sympathize with me and declare that that made for a few difficult days. The point is that though weaning can be a rough process, it's healthy.

The child will eventually learn, to his or her surprise, that table food meets all health needs. Mother's milk is no longer needed. After the process is complete, the child may crawl up in that same lap of the mother and love on her, not even thinking of the nursing that he or she had just recently cried over as if it were a life-and-death matter. That's a cute memory in babies, but a rather ugly one in pilgrims. Still, the end of the process is beautiful in both cases.

We too need the process of being weaned from pride and ambition so that we can realize that the table food of submitting to God's tastes great and satisfies. We must come to the place where His will moves our hearts like our ambition once did! David doesn't fuss and fret here because he's quieted like a baby weaned recently from his mother's milk. Mother's milk was natural in the former situation but is not healthy to continue for all of life. Likewise, just as pride and ambition are part of our sinful race, they are most unhealthy to have control of our lives. Notice that the phrase is repeated here for emphasis, but the words *"my soul"* are added. The problem is deep, and so must be the weaning.

III. What It Means for the Future (V. 3)

A. Hoping

Does verse 3 sound familiar? Notice how it compares to Psalm 130:7. It's that strong Bible hope. It's an encouraging hope as there was absolutely no hope in his former pride and ambition. As with anyone who progresses with pride and ambition, David now thinks of others. Israel needs the same sort of help and hope, as do we all. Israel had trouble with never seeing anything but herself while the Lord meant for her to be a light to the whole world. Israel, as well as you and me, can look to the Lord – there is hope!

B. Trust

We read *"from henceforth and forever"*. God's will can give us what pride and ambition never could. The only real way to be in *"great matters"* is to be in the Lord's will because nothing is *"too high"* for Him! Strangely, we crave being important while our faith says only Christ is important. The trajectory of our lives denies what we claim to stand for!

Don't jump into *"things too high for me"* as that is not a lofty goal for life. To be sure, His plan may include obscurity or apparent failure, the very things that devastate our pride and ambition, but it will still be a great plan. Do you notice here that he never mentions all he hopes for? The Lord's plan is great, but we don't yet know it all. In that case, pilgrim, we need weaned from our pride and ambition to learn to trust and thrill in His plan. We must unload this burden and get on to God's presence like these pilgrims heading to Jerusalem. Let us leave to the Lord these *"things too high for me"*.

14

Lord, Remember

Psalm 132

Have you ever wondered after years of counting on the Lord and His promises if He would really bring it all the pass in the end? Even worse, have you worried if all you've depended on wouldn't work out at all? These pilgrims in Israel have seen the Lord perform great things in David and make great promises to Israel through him. In their nervous doubts, they pray, "*Lord, remember*".

I. The People Pray (v. 1-10)

A. Remembering David's Dedication

The burden the pilgrim needs to unload in this instance in going to the Lord's presence is nagging fears about the promises of God. In what is by far the longest of the Pilgrim Psalms, and in one that is also known as a Royal Psalm, this Psalm in some ways summarizes all 15 of these Pilgrim Psalms. We shouldn't be surprised by its length as it's no wonder that such time is taken to thoroughly go through what the pilgrim struggles with. The design of this Psalm is special too. Verses 1-10 rehearses David's vow to God with a prayer for the pilgrim to hold on to what David believed while verses 11-18 reviews the Lord's vow to David with the Lord answering that prayer.

Many believe this Psalm was either related to David's life or was from early in Solomon's life after the great dedication of the Temple was over and people were wondering if the Lord would carry on the greatness that had been shown. The way David is being looked back to, and the fact that the Temple dedication seems to have already happened and seeing how a portion of Solomon's prayer in II Chronicles 6:41-42 is quoted in verses 8-10, makes me believe this Psalm is dated to Solomon's days.

These pilgrims were aware of the promise the Lord had made to David in II Samuel 7:16: *"And thine house and thy kingdom shall be established for ever before thee: thy throne shall be established for ever."* These pilgrims were depending on that promise more than we can realize. Enemies surrounded their borders and world news they received from travelers was often bleak. As they dwell on that promise to David here while now inside the gates of Jerusalem, and as they're thinking of so many things in their lives, they pray, *"Lord, remember"*.

The prayer *"Lord, remember"* is one of both worry and faith. It's worry in that they're really praying, "don't forget, Lord". It's faith in that they're also praying, "I know You'll remember, Lord". Despite the mingled worry and faith, this prayer has the pilgrim saying that he knows that if the Lord remembers His promises all will be well. We Christian pilgrims should agree that if He keeps His promises to us all will be well too. Considering their specific promises, they pray, *"Lord, remember David"*. In our case, I agree with Spurgeon who said we should pray, "Lord, remember Jesus". As you know, of course, all our promises are in Him! As it turns out, these ancient pilgrims look to Jesus as well, as this Psalm will labor to show. The only difference we have with the pilgrim in this psalm is that their light is less than ours.

When the pilgrim adds *"and all his afflictions"*, he expands his thoughts to David's dedication. In no way is he saying that the Lord owed David and for that reason the Lord must keep the promise, but rather that David believed the promise and taught us well here where we weary pilgrims struggle with doubts. The promises of God carried David through his sufferings with Saul and several other life episodes. David lived resting on the promises.

David swore and vowed to the *"mighty God of Jacob"*. Perhaps Jacob is mentioned rather than Abraham and Isaac because Jacob was known for making a vow. Because David so believed the promises, he was moved to honor and glorify the Lord. II Samuel 7:1-2 (*"And it came to pass, when the king sat in his house, and the LORD had given him rest round about from all his enemies; That the king said unto Nathan the prophet, See now, I dwell in an house of cedar, but the ark of God dwelleth within curtains."*) records that David was bothered that he had a nice home while the Lord and His Ark didn't. Verses 3-4 show us how David lost interest in his home and couldn't enjoy it, nor even sleep, till the Lord had His House.

God's House became David's passion in his later life. He was so interested in the Temple that it took prominence over all other projects in his life. In our day, some act is if they wouldn't care if God's house of worship, the local church, collapsed. We need to channel David's attitude.

In a way, the pilgrim here relates what pilgrims struggle with in all these Pilgrim Psalms – there must be a place for the Lord's presence. David echoes what these Pilgrim Psalms repeatedly teach us – the Lord must have His "*place*" and we pilgrims can have no less than His presence. Along those lines, the word "*habitation*" is used three times in this Psalm and is a key word meaning dwelling place or residence.[13] Repetition of the phrase "*mighty God of Jacob*" highlights that the Lord is Almighty, and yet we can and must have His presence. We see two things here working out the issue of God keeping His promises: heritage and fellowship. We have great promises (heritage) and need God's presence to be confident of those promises (fellowship).

B. Remembering the Ark and Worship

By David's time, the Tabernacle and Ark were almost forgotten, or at least grossly neglected. Unlike others of his time, David sought them. While in Ephratah, which is another name for his boyhood home of Bethlehem, he heard of the Ark, but by the time he got to see it he found it in "*the fields of the wood*". That place is the woody area of Kirjath-Jearim where the Ark spent 20

---

[13] The three times are verses 5 and 13 as "*habitation*" and verse 7 where the word is rendered "*tabernacles*".

years after the Philistines returned it after they had taken it in battle. As you recall, the Lord punished the Philistines for taking it in the first place. Where you would think the people of Israel would have been overjoyed to have it back, they still let it be neglected in *"the fields of the wood"*. How unbecoming was that neglect for a God so mighty and Whose presence was so needed!

In verses 6 and 7, the plural pronoun *"we"* begins to be used. Apparently, David's zeal for the presence of the Lord motivated others. In verse 7, the mention of *"tabernacles"* suggests that the Lord can't be confined to the Temple that is less than even His footstool, which is the whole earth.

I love what is said here of David and the pilgrims. Can you see it? It almost jumps off the page and demands a response:

We found it;

We will go;

We will worship.

We pilgrims of today need this same experience. We should find God's presence because it can be found. We should go to it because it's so worth going. We should worship Him because He is so worthy of our worship.

By verse 8 they are paraphrasing Numbers 10:35 (*"And it came to pass, when the ark set forward, that Moses said, Rise up, LORD, and let thine enemies be scattered; and let them that hate thee flee before thee."*) that was used each time the Ark was moved. Remember the Lord dwelt in that moving Tabernacle, but David desires the Lord in a constant place where He can be found. For the record, both the moving Tabernacle and the constant Temple picture what the Lord does for us. The Lord moves with us yet is always found in the same place! In our day, neither the Tabernacle nor the Temple are in use, but the need to crave finding His presence still exists.

It's as if this Psalm is saying, let a believing congregation come forward. *"Priests"* (verses 9 and 16) and *"clothed"* (verses 9,

16, and 18) become important. The idea is that priests serve in the Temple clothed with righteousness, or at least that's how it's supposed to be. Episodes in Israel's history like the unrighteous sons of Eli serving in the Tabernacle were seen as the gross anomaly that they were. In the same way, we Christian pilgrims are each a priest clothed in Christ's righteousness. With promises of this caliber, no wonder the pilgrims pray, "*and let thy saints shout for joy*" in this prayer that begun "*Lord, remember*". In verse 10 the plea for David's "*anointed*" is a look forward to the greater David, Jesus Christ. Yes, let's pray, "*Lord, remember*".

II. The People Remember the Lord

A. Remembering God's Promises

Beginning in verse 11, the Lord responds with His side of the covenant with David and answers the prayer that was made in verses 1-10. This answer from the Lord is one that the pilgrims will gladly sing, especially if they have that stray thought of wondering if the Lord will keep His promises. It is at this point that the shocking lesson of this Psalm appears before our eyes. It turns out that the answer for "*Lord, remember*" is that we remember the Lord. Who would've thought that simply flipping the prayer around would have been its answer?

We would do well to remember that these promises are from the God Who cannot lie. Notice that it says, "*he will not turn*". That phrase is mentioned twice in verses 11-12 to remind us that He isn't leading us along. In our saner moments, we know that He will never fail us, nor forget His promises. In verse 2 David swore, but in verse 11 the Lord does and that is far better. In fact, that's rock solid.

Those promises are so far-reaching that he says, "*of the fruit of thy body will I set up on thy throne*". David's line will continue. With what we know of what happened to David's throne in the Babylonian Captivity, what does this statement mean? Luke 2:4 ("*And Joseph also went up from Galilee, out of the city of Nazareth, into Judaea, unto the city of David, which is called Bethlehem; (because he was of the house and lineage of David:)*") provides the clue. David's line will be continued by Jesus Christ, the greater Son of David. Christ fulfills promises in Himself!

B. Remembering the Lord's Way

Verse 12 reminds us that the Lord expects things of His children and will bring in chastening where needed. Though that chastening may complicate our lives, He will keep His promises. Verse 13 suggests natural questions. Why do we wonder if He will keep His promises? Or why do we wonder if living for Christ will be worth it? The answer is simple. He chose Israel and loved her first. He chose to love all people, pilgrim, before we ever loved Him. He loved first and with the greatest intensity and that's the best proof He'll keep His promises.

III. The Lord Remembers the People (V. 14-18)

A. Remembering to Provide

This Psalm turns even more incredible as the Lord now interrupts to speak directly to the pilgrim Himself! (Notice *"I"* and *"my"* the rest of the way). When the Lord says, *"this is my rest"*, the word *"rest"* refers to a resting place. It's quite like the word *"habitations"*, but with a restful connotation. For the Lord, that rest is all tied up in His people and it is *"for ever"*. He is saying that I will dwell with you and keep My Word. In fact, He's saying, I passionately desire it!

We pilgrims should notice in verse 15 that this not only speaks of the far-off promise, but He is saying too, I will keep you now. This is His promise of provision and bread. How we forget, worrying pilgrim, that He already keeps His promises every day! He even throws in the word *"abundantly"* to show us that His keeping us is beyond mere sustenance.

Notice how verse 16 proves that He not only kept His promises, but He listened carefully to our prayers. In verse 9 we prayed for the priest to be clothed with righteousness and here they are clothed with salvation. In verse 9 we prayed that the saints would shout for joy and here they do. The only difference is that the word *"aloud"* is added. We can now verbally proclaim it as it's already a kept promise.

B. Remembering Forever

We prayed *"Lord, remember"* and now look where verses 17 and 18 bring us. We are told that the Lord will *"make the horn of David to bud"*. *"Horn"* here speaks of power, strength, and honor while the idea of *"bud"* is that it will sprout and grow. The promises of David, then, bud and grow even greater in Christ. That was true in Christ's First Coming and will be even more evident in the Millennium.

The Lord then says, *"I have ordained a lamp for mine anointed"*. A *"lamp"* is a symbol of ongoing light. We have been told that David was a lamp, for example in II Samuel 21:17, but the word *"anointed"* also means that this speaks more particularly of Christ. As pitch-black as all seems now in our darkened world, so dark that we sometimes doubt Him keeping His promises, the Lord still has a lamp to enlighten and keep those promises! No wonder we say this Psalm summarizes all the Pilgrim Psalms as in it Christ is most clearly revealed as the answer to the problems of pilgrims.

Verse 18 gives us another profound reason why we should not worry about the Lord keeping, or failing to keep, His promises. Pilgrim, we are the wrong ones to be worrying. It's the enemies of David, or the enemies of the Lord, who had better worry that the Lord will keep His promises! As it turns out, they are the only ones with anything to worry about. The contrast between we pilgrims and them is striking – look how shame contrasts with the crown. Pilgrim, we won't have the charred, mangled crowns of Hell, but the glorious, jeweled ones of Heaven! The promises are true! We will walk the streets of gold and look upon His face! Considering that destination, we pilgrims need not worry. Let's release the burden of unfounded fears and pray and sing in faith: *"Lord, remember"*.

15

Unity

Psalm 133

Have you ever really experienced the refreshing closeness of God's people where all love the Lord and are on the same page? Sadly, many Christians rarely get that experience. The Pilgrim here knows how broken unity can so trouble you and really cloud your mind when it's time to go to the Lord's presence. It's as if the pilgrim here sings of what we need and will sing it until the need is met. That need is *"unity"*.

I. The Pleasantness of Unity (v. 1)

A. It Is Good

The Pilgrim is here, and the beauties of Jerusalem are all around him. He looks at the Temple doors to which he has so far traveled. It's time to come into the presence of the Lord. But wait! There's still an obstacle that must be dealt with before he enters those Temple doors. He must unload this burden, or he will not experience the Lord's presence in the great way intended. His problem? Unity is disrupted.

That this problem would come so near the end of the Pilgrim Psalms is no surprise. The pilgrim is in the city thronged with fellow pilgrims. That should be a glorious thing as they gather for the same reason of worshiping the same God. Nothing should ever call for more unity than worshiping the same Lord. Because they believe the same Lord, they believe so many of the same things.

Despite all that basis for unity, we know, pilgrims then and now, lose it as easily as chocolate chip cookies disappear off the kitchen table. You see, this pilgrim has traveled closely with other pilgrims for many miles. They've spent many hours in travel and in camp. No doubt campsites were kept tight for extra security on the trail. They were likely almost tripping over each other. Aggravations accumulate easily, nerves get frayed, and all kinds of conflict rob the joy of the Lord Whose presence they together travel to. Again, there's no shock that this was one of the later complications for the pilgrim traveling to God's presence.

"*Behold*" immediately grabs our attention. It's worth taking notice of this troubling issue. As we said before, the approach to dealing with it will be about singing the ideal of unity until it is appealing again. No issue that broke unity is mentioned as such reasons are so rarely worth mentioning. We go straight to the positive beauty of unity.

This psalm is a "*song of degrees of David*". That the Lord picked David to pen this Psalm on the great need of unity is of no surprise either. David had seen firsthand the devastation of disunity. Whether it was when his brothers misjudged him and got angry when he came to fight Goliath, or all those years of conflict with Saul, or the treachery of Absalom stealing his kingdom, David has lived disunity.

We realize that although this Psalm concentrates on our worshiping the Lord together (corporately), it's no discredit to private worship, but rather a companion to it. While they had the Temple, we have the local church and assembling together is still the Lord's plan. As Hebrews 10:25 says, "*Not forsaking the assembling of ourselves together, as the manner of some is; but exhorting one another: and so much the more, as ye see the day approaching.*"

Unity is at once expected and essential to corporate worship. No wonder it says here "*how good and how pleasant it is*".[14] May

---

[14] "*Good*" and "*pleasant*" are often paired with each other in the Old Testament. See Genesis 49:15, Psalm 147:1, Job 36:11, and Proverbs 24:25.

the Lord help us to never underestimate or forget its incredible pleasantness. One way we know that this is true is by how bad and unpleasant it is without unity. Many of us have ugly memories that dot the stories of our lives. Yes, we know how good and pleasant unity is and how rotten disunity is.

The scope of this truth is broad. When it says *"brethren"* here it reminds us that this principle reaches beyond the Temple or the local church to the Christian family, or a circle of Christian friends, or Christian neighbors or coworkers! We, pilgrims then or Christians now, are children of an incredible Father and have great things in common in Jesus Christ. Considering that fact, unity is the most natural thing in the world.

B. The Dwelling Together

While *"to dwell together"* is the starting point, it alone is no more than close contact. A big family, for example, could dwell together, but not have unity at all. There's eight of us that live under my roof, and some days we have unity while other days we merely dwell together. *"Unity"* is the key in this discussion and goes far beyond just physical closeness. Further, to be at odds with a Christian brother or sister is an incredible hindrance to being in God's presence.

"Unity" means to be joined as a unit and suggests the idea of oneness or being in concord. The pilgrim will naturally ask what qualifies as unity and how far does it go. Unity is sometimes misunderstood to mean agreeing at all costs, but that's not the unity meant here if we mean no more than going for the least common denominator. That approach will cause us to toss out Christ, His Word, and the blood atonement! Those treasures are at once the foundation and the building blocks of our unity. In other words, we unify around Christ and what He gives us. These are the things that take us to *"heavenly places"* and make unity the good and pleasant thing that it is.

Unity does not imply uniformity. Despite what many say, they are not interchangeable synonyms. We may each have a different favorite color, but we all have the same Savior, Jesus Christ! In that case, we lack uniformity but have wonderful unity. I read somewhere an analogy that really helps me grasp this idea. Think of a symphony. In a symphony, you have all different instruments joined around a common piece of music, and within the confines of the musical score, each does his or her best to add to it. That's beautiful unity. Uniformity would be everyone playing the same instrument in the entire symphony. Would 50 trumpets sound as good as a full symphony to you? No, and neither is uniformity good and pleasant as unity.

We are to seek unity without demanding uniformity. We pilgrims are part of Christ's body, but we have differing gifts, which is a thought that the New Testament expands (I Corinthians 12:4-6). We pilgrims today can take the New Testament and remember too that the Body has different parts, but the same Head – Jesus Christ! The New Testament uses the term "fellowship", but the idea is the same as unity for pilgrims then or now.

II. The Fragrance of Unity (v. 2)

A. It Is Precious

Two metaphors are given to illustrate the beauty of unity. The first one involves oil. We realize that olive oil is already a precious ointment for all in that hot, dry climate that is so detrimental to the skin, but the oil here goes all the way back to Exodus where Aaron was anointed the High Priest (Exodus 29:9; 30:22, 25, 30). That oil is called *"precious"*, which turns out to be the same word as *"good"* in verse 1. In fact, it's the same word the Lord used in Genesis when he described His creation as *"good"*. With that comparison, we can see just how good and precious this unity is.

The special mixture in the oil that was used to anoint Aaron was known for emitting a wonderful fragrance. That smell reminded Israel of how the Lord unified them back when He graciously anointed Aaron on their behalf. For we pilgrims today, oil is a picture of the Holy Spirit. We, too, have an even greater High Priest in Jesus Christ. For the record, Jesus was anointed by the Holy Spirit (I John 2:20,27). We, then, can see why Aaron was such a special symbol of unity in his anointing.

B. The Running Down

The picture here of unity is that the consecrating oil poured on top of Aaron's head ran down over him. First, it went down and covered his beard. His beard is mentioned twice to show the thoroughness of the coverage of this oil. Next, the oil continued down onto *"the skirts of his garments"*. That would refer to his collar and mean that it covered his collar and went down profusely on to his clothes. It's easy to visualize the lavish amounts of oil pouring down on Aaron.

Notice this oil was first poured on Aaron's head just as the Holy Spirit was poured on Christ, Who is our Head. A further key to understanding this matter is noticing the usages of *"ran down"*, *"went down"*, and *"descended"*, which are all the same word in their Hebrew language. It's an ironic lesson we learn in this Song of Ascents. When we ascend to Jerusalem, or to the presence of the Lord, what we need comes down. This lesson of pilgrims going up to receive what comes down is one of the greatest principles of these Pilgrim Psalms.

Following the Lord in unity will give impressive benefits towards the Lord's presence. This all came down so abundantly that it covered his head (hair), beard, and clothes, meaning that these distinctions were covered by it. You see, unity covers differences with God's love! The balance to the foundational basis of unity around the Person of Jesus Christ is love.

The truth of unity, then, is so profound that we should despise divisiveness, gossip, unforgiveness, fights, debates over trivial things, and cliques. We should be disgusted by these things and see them as destructive to unity, devastating to our spiritual lives, and as detours away from God's presence. We aren't the same, but we have the same Bible, the same beliefs on the Person of Jesus

Christ, so we should have unity. In Christ, we have all that's needed for unity.

What, then, is the greatest enemy of unity? The love of self. I can't love my fellow pilgrims because I'm thinking only of my needs. I can't love the congregation I assemble with because I'm so consumed with myself. My petty feelings have become greater than the group. Even worse, those selfish feelings have become greater to me than the glory of Jesus Christ. Isn't it clear for any pilgrim how this sabotages our going into the presence of the Lord?

III. The Refreshing Nature of Unity (v. 3)

A. It Is God-Given

In verse 3 we turn to a new analogy, but the point remains unity. The lesson that it's not about us agreeing with each other perfectly, but the idea of receiving it from above remains as well. First, we are told about *"the dew of Hermon"*. Dew is prolific on Mount Hermon, which is a 9000-foot peak at Israel's northernmost border. Next, we are told of the dew on *"the mountains of Zion"*. Zion, of course, refers to Jerusalem where both precipitation and dew are not as abundant as on Hermon.

This analogy is quite instructive on unity as well. From far away (Hermon) all the way to Jerusalem God's blessing of dew falls. As is always the case in these Pilgrim Psalms, the direction is always toward Jerusalem where God's presence can be reached. Unity should cover the whole journey. In other words, unity must cover all or it will be compromised. As we have probably all experienced, just a few uncovered spots in unity can wreak havoc.

Hermon is a far greater (bigger) mountain than Zion and had more dew as well, but God's blessing of unity covers the greater and the lesser. That is always God's design. When we see the word *"descended"* we are again reminded that it comes down from God. We are also being called on to have unity and at the same time to always remember where it comes from.

The point about this dew that mustn't be missed is that it is so refreshing. Especially on Zion as there would be no rain six months out of each year. During that rainless time, dew was incredibly refreshing. Refreshing – isn't that what you want, pilgrim? This lack of unity isn't refreshing, but exhausting and contrary to God's presence. Look up to the Lord and it will come down to you.

B. The Blessing Evermore

In the last part of verse 3 that says, *"for there the Lord commanded the blessing"*, the word *"there"* is emphatic. Where is *"there"*? For the pilgrims in this Psalm, it was Jerusalem. But if that's the case for us, let's all go catch a plane. God's presence was specifically in Jerusalem in those days but is now available anywhere. Still, *"there"* can only be reached via the road of *"unity"*. *"There"* turns out to be the place of blessing. *"Blessing"* is a key Old Testament term that still thrills the hearts of pilgrims today. It's a place we all want to be, but we can't get there without *"unity"*. *"There"* – what a place!

What is *"unity"*? Ultimately, it's unhindered Christian love. Look where else it goes. It leads to *"even life for evermore"*. In this case, that's not speaking of everlasting life, but of God's amazing blessing. Men have always sought riches, or a fountain of youth, or some elixir, but that's not our need. We simply need the blessing, and the watchword of that life is *"unity"*.

Think of it! A trumpet will sound, and God's people will assemble in the clouds. See, we are unified in something, or should I say, Someone. That unity will carry into Heaven and the eternal ages! Let's, then, take on unity now and get used to it. If we don't, we pilgrims will slump and stay back from God's presence now. O Lord, help us pilgrims to have *"unity"*.

16

Bless the Lord

Psalm 134

What is it like to truly be in the presence of the Lord? Can we talk intelligently about it from experience, or can we only regurgitate what everyone else says? Is it only an emotional feeling, or is there more to it? Does the Bible describe for us what it will be like? In this final Pilgrim Psalm, with the pilgrims finally at their destination, we will see when they proclaim: *"bless the LORD"*.

I. Bless the Lord in Service (v. 1)

A. The Call to Servants

They made it. They've traveled many hard miles from their homes throughout Israel and now they are on the Temple steps entering in. They've dealt with many issues along the way in the previous 14 Psalms that hindered them from seeking the presence of the Lord, but they've turned to the Lord, and you might say have sung their way out of it. Can you imagine their feelings? They slap each other on the back and proclaim: we made it! Their hearts are deeply rejoicing.

This place is also where we would hope the 15 Pilgrim Psalms would end – in Jerusalem and in His presence. Press on, pilgrim; it's possible to reach His presence. For them, it's been the long journey from *"woe is me"* in Psalm 122 to *"bless the LORD"* here. There's no time for solos here in this last Pilgrim song as the choir is jubilant.

Some of these psalms, particularly, have focused on coming to the Lord's presence as a group and this is another one much of that variety, though the private presence of the Lord would have many similarities to what is discussed here. Most believe, and I agree, that the first two verses are the pilgrim singing out to those who serve in the Temple while verse 3 is those servants answering back to the pilgrims.

We see a distinction here. In this Psalm, there are clearly the pilgrims who are arriving and the servants who are already there. In a sense, all Christians are pilgrims, yet on the other hand, there are those who serve in the corporate worship distinct from the pilgrims traveling in. This does not suggest that there are two tiers of Christians, but it does highlight that those who serve have added responsibilities. In other words, the pilgrims traveling in have expectations about the pilgrims who are already serving there.

It's as if the joyous pilgrims arriving are crying out to the servants, "*bless the LORD*" and don't mess this up. Servants in the public worship of the Lord need to remember this very legitimate request. Priests and Levites did various functions in the Temple just like a pastor and others serve in a local church. As a pastor, I understand the people's right to ask me not to mess this up and to "*bless the LORD*". Remember, we bless the Lord by giving Him His just praise and honor.

Though a pastor in our day corresponds well here, a pastor is not all that would be in mind. The Levites didn't do what the priests did, but still the pilgrims cried out: "*all ye servants of the LORD*". In a local church, there's deacons, musicians, teachers, and all kinds of behind-the-scenes workers who are all contributing to the worthy worship of the Lord. Even the most menial tasks in the Temple were essential to the worship honoring the Lord. It's all important!

It's best we all serve in the local church and remember that all the other pilgrims are depending on us to "*bless the LORD*" and enrich the experience of being in the Lord's presence for all. With this reality in view, there's no place for self-glory, or arguing, or selfishness, or man worship. We must worship Him, or as it says here, *"bless the LORD"*.

B. The Call to Stand

Notice that of the servants it says: *"which by night stand"*. The thought is not only do they serve correctly, but more importantly, do they do it faithfully. How do you know if your service is both right and faithful? It's a simple test really. Just ask, does it *"bless the LORD"*? 1 Chronicles 9:33 says, *"And these are the singers, chief of the fathers of the Levites, who remaining in the chambers were free: for they were employed in that work day and night."* Amazingly, they kept the Temple where praise to the Lord was constantly offered up.

The word *"stand"* is often used of the work of the priests and Levites. It is our New Testament call as well. For example, Ephesians 6:13 says, *"... and having done all, to stand"*. Remember also, that the New Testament plea is for us to *"... be instant in season, out of season"*. We hope our church is alive more than three times a week, but as a church that has three services a week we have these three special opportunities to worship the Lord. May we strive to make sure in each of these opportunities that we *"bless the LORD"*.

An additional benefit of this Psalm is that it removes any illusions about His presence. The word *"stand"* also means to minister, and so we are speaking of faithful service to the Lord. Can't you see it? We never need to stop service to the Lord to find His presence. In fact, we find it in faithfulness <u>as</u> we *"bless the LORD"*. The word *"night"* reminds us that just as the work never stopped in the Temple, it may be some dark hour of life that your service is most needed. That difficult place may be where you most effectively *"bless the LORD"*. As you come to His presence, stay faithful, serve Him from a heart that loves Him, and remember to *"bless the LORD"*.

II. Bless the Lord in Prayer and Praise (v. 2)

A. The Call to Pray

Verse 2 contains a request for "*all*" servants. I pray that each of us, pilgrims, are both in the category of servant and Pilgrim. If you're a believer, of course, you're a pilgrim in this world, but hopefully you have jumped into the category of servant as well.

"*Lift up your hands*" is a reference to prayer. Prayer is needed both on the way and in the presence of the Lord as surely you will use that presence to commune with Him. Psalms 28:2 says, "*Hear the voice of my supplications, when I cry unto thee, when I lift up my hands toward thy holy oracle*". We know that believers in the Old Testament used a few different prayer postures. They would kneel, which is more in line with what we are used to, or even fall flat on their faces in a sign of deep humility. Another common one would be where they would hold up their hands toward Heaven and pray. The idea there is that we are reaching up to God from where our help comes when we lift empty hands for Him to fill. It was considered an acknowledgment that the Lord has heard and will continue to hear our prayer. The practice even continued into the New Testament.[15]

In our day, some might hold up their hands in worship services, for example, in music. If the uplifted hands only meant that I enjoyed being entertained, they would not correspond to what we have here. But if the presence of the Lord moved our hearts to turn the words of the song into prayer it would be like what we have here. We are not, of course, required to hold up our hands in worship, but turning the words into a prayer to our Lord would be a fantastic thing.

Remember, our hearts and thoughts must be toward the Lord, and in spirit we who come to God's presence in the local church can turn upward to Him in singing, giving offering, listening to singing, and especially in taking in His precious Word. As you may be

---

[15] An example would be 1 Timothy 2:8.

starting to see, terms like "God's presence", "fellowship", and "worship" overlap well.

B. The Call to Praise

Notice that verse 2 repeats "*bless the LORD*". The original meaning of the word "*bless*" was to kneel. That definition certainly fits when we think about our blessing the Lord. The word further means to enrich. That the Lord ever does for us, but how do we "*bless*" Him? How could we bless Him if blessing means to enrich? It's easy to say, "*bless the LORD*", but how is it done? Well, most importantly, we know that our blessing the Lord and Him blessing us is going to have to look different. Very different!

I can't bless or enrich the Lord Who owns all, but I can offer the praise due His name. That praise is how you "*bless the LORD*". While that might include things like words or singing, it involves more as well. We can selflessly serve and give of ourselves, such as we are, as He taught us and for His glory. That blesses the Lord. Remember people can ignore these realities of blessing the Lord and come to some Christian music and sway and lift hands but have no interest in blessing the Lord. It's not blessing the Lord unless it springs forth from a sincere, faithful, obedient, worshiping heart. In the real and close way that the pilgrims sought here, let's "*bless the LORD*".

III. Now in Turn, Blessed by the Lord (v.3)

A. The Response of Belief

As we said before, this last verse is where the servants answer back in song to these arriving pilgrims. What a scene! Unity present and obstacles to God's presence faced and dealt with, and now "*the LORD that made heaven and earth bless thee out of Zion*". Always keep the grandeur of the Lord before you in His presence – He is "*the LORD that made heaven and earth*".

Do you wonder if the Lord can bless you? Is this something that He still does? Do you find yourself entertaining the thought of whether His presence is really worth the effort or not? Hold on – He is the LORD, the mighty Creator! In these Pilgrim Psalms, we are always taken back to His Person and His traits. No matter the obstacle to the Lord's presence that the pilgrim faces, we are always pulled back toward the Lord and His splendid character. Dwell on that pilgrim, and your outlook will change. The Lord sustains all and is Who we need. Even better, the Lord will commune with us.

B. The Response of Blessing

Have you noticed the two keywords of this Psalm? You will find these two words used in all three verses. The words are "*LORD*" and "*bless*". The word "*bless*", however, changes for the pilgrim from a word of giving to one of receiving. The words "*bless thee*" suggest that the blessing is now coming back the pilgrim's way.

The blessing the pilgrim now receives reminds us of the more detailed blessing given in Moses' time. Numbers 6:22-26 says, "*And the LORD spake unto Moses, saying, Speak unto Aaron and unto his sons, saying, On this wise ye shall bless the children of Israel, saying unto them, The LORD bless thee, and keep thee: The LORD make his face shine upon thee, and be gracious unto thee: The LORD lift up his countenance upon thee, and give thee peace.*" The Lord, you see, has been blessing for a long time.

The priest who blesses the Lord as these pilgrims asked now blesses the people. The blessing they pronounce is the blessing of the Lord. Though this pronouncement was made to a group of pilgrims, the word "*thee*" speaks of a unified congregation with blessing for every individual. All any of us can really do is ask the Lord to bless others. It is the Lord Who has the endless bounty.

"*The LORD*" puts it in perspective. We wait for blessing; we need He Who blesses (the LORD). Notice that we are to be blessed "*out of Zion*". Zion is where the Lord's presence is. For them that is Jerusalem, but for us it's not a location. Zion reminds us that all blessing can only come from where the Lord's blessing is, and that is in Himself.

Pilgrim, as was true in all 15 of these Pilgrim Psalms, never settle for anything less than the Lord's presence. Seek His presence corporately and in private and always make it your highest goal. Unload the things that need unloading because they hinder you from His presence, and as you go, be sure to *"bless the LORD"*.

17

Conclusion

The Pilgrim Psalms take us on one of the most important journeys of the Christian life. It's an arduous journey with many twists, turns, cliffs, obstacles, grand views, and dark valleys. It's a trek that very few people encourage you to take, or a climb that very few even think worth the sweat and muscle cramps, yet it's a golden pathway that the Lord almost begs you to take in these psalms. It's the path to His presence.

Our pilgrimage is a journey. Difficulties are repetitive. Errors are repeated. New episodes of life require a fresh journey to the Lord's presence. Remember, the pilgrims of Israel left home three times a year to make these difficult journeys to the Lord's presence in Jerusalem. I'm glad the trip is not now so long because I've come to see that I'm going to need the journey far more than three times a year!

If I live long enough, I'm going to be slandered again, be overwhelmed in trouble again, be afraid and need help again, be joyless again, be swirling in worries over my family again, be afflicted again, be selfishly ambitious and fail again, be involved in worship and unity problems again, and likely be found "*in the depths*" again. Actually, I probably won't have to live very long to go through all of them again. In fact, I'm surprised at how often I've cycled through these types of issues, and yet I'm amazed at the Lord's grace in helping me every single time I turn to Him. I'm saddened by how far in the depths I've fallen before but praise His name for the fact that I was never farther than His hand could reach. I'm thankful He ever seeks, and that He will never cease seeking us. To that end, He has even given treasures like these Pilgrim Psalms to encourage us to continue seeking His presence

Is the Lord's purpose for giving us the Pilgrim Psalms becoming clearer? What we might mistakenly conclude in our first study of these psalms is that if we study and grasp them, we can get beyond such problems. As it turns out, that is not the Lord's purpose at all. His purpose is that these psalms become the template for problems I'm going to see again and again. Since I'm likely going to fail again and again as well, these psalms can teach me to run more quickly to the only real solution for such problems – the presence of my Lord. Every time the Pilgrim Psalms compel me to run to my Lord's presence will serve as proof that the luster of these precious gemstones has reached my heart.

Made in United States
Troutdale, OR
01/13/2024

16931900R00076